How To Become A United States Citizen

A Step-by-Step Guidebook for Self Instruction

Fourth Edition

Como Hacerse Ciudadano De Los Estados Unidos

Una Guía Detallada de Auto-Instrucción

Cuarta Edición

General Studies - ESL

by
Sally Abel Schreuder

Nolo Press - Occidental

P. O. Box 722, Occidental, CA 95465

(707) 874-3105

Printing History

First Edition	July 1983
Second Printing	October 1984
Second Edition	August 1986
Third Edition	January 1988
Second Printing	June 1988
Third Printing	October 1988
Fourth Printing	April 1989
Fourth Edition	January 1992

Credits

Spanish translation: Martha Oberti
Spanish updates: Roberto Lozano
Cover and illustrations: Janet Kirwan Madison

ISBN: 0-944508-10-3
Library of Congress Catalog No. 83-062116

Dedication

This book is dedicated to my daddy, Johannes Wilhelmus Brand, who at age twenty, in 1923, immigrated to the United States. He came from Holland on a boat called the "New Amsterdam" in search of the American dream...and he found it! He lived the rest of his life as a proud American citizen, never taking America for granted. It was his example that prompted me to teach classes helping hundreds of aliens to become United States citizens and finally, to write this self-help book. May many more immigrants, like my dad, fully experience America, the land of opportunity, through United States citizenship.

Acknowledgment

We are deeply indebted to **Dan P. Danilov**, a noted immigration attorney in Seattle, Washington, for his many valuable suggestions and for his enthusiastic support throughout this project.

Mr. Danilov has practiced in the immigration law field for over 30 years. He is author of the prestigious law book, **Danilov's U.S. Immigration Law Citator** and has been editor for various immigration law journals. Time taken from such a busy professional life to help with this book was an act of real generosity for which we are truly grateful.

CONTENIDO

TABLE OF CONTENTS

APÉNDICE

APPENDICES

LISTA DE EJEMPLARES

Numero	Formulario	
1	N-400	Solicitud para Iniciar la Petición de Naturalización
2	G-325	Formulario de Informe Biográfico
3	N-402	Solicitud para Iniciar la Petición de Naturalización a nombre de un niño.
4	N-600	Solicitud para Certificado de Ciudadanía
5		Una carta como ejemplo para Obtener una Solicitud
6	N-400	Instrucciones para el solicitante
7	N-405	Petición de Naturalización
8	N-445	El Aviso de Comparecencia para la Audiencia Final
9	N-565	Solicitud de una Naturalización Nueva o Papel de Ciudadaniá
10		Solicitud de pasaporte
11		Tarjeta de Empadranamiento

LIST OF SAMPLES

Introducción

El objeto de este libro es ayudarlo a que usted mismo pueda completar solo el procedimiento de hacerse Ciudadano de los Estados Unidos. Ya que éste es un libro de auto-ayuda completo, ud. se puede preparar para la ciudadanía en la conveniencia y la comodidad de su hogar, cuando ud. tenga el tiempo disponible y a su propio paso. Ejemplares de formularios que se usan para lograrlo se le han incluido para guiarlo.

El procedimiento de naturalización, comenzando desde el momento de llenar la solicitud y terminando con la audiencia donde toma ud. el juramento de fidelidad, puede tomar un mínimode unos meses o un máximode casi dos años. Una espera de un año aproximadamente no es nada raro. La mayoría del tiempo, la solicitud está fuera de sus manos y se va tramitando por los oficiales federales. Asi es que es mejor comenzar inmediatamente, tan pronto como sea ud. calificado. Entre más pronto comience, más pronto se hará ud. un ciudadano.

Nota

La intención de este libro es de proveer información correcta y autorizada referente al procedimiento de la naturalización para la ciudadanía de los Estados Unidos. Todo cuidado se ha tomado para escribirlo, y los individuos necesarios y las materias de referencia apropiadas se han consultado, especialmente ésas del Servicio de Inmigración y Naturalización del Departamento de Justicia de los Estados Unidos. Sin embargo, las leyes federales sobre la naturalización pueden ser cambiadas. Así es que, para tener un informe detallado y al tanto, especialmente en casos complejos, el solicitante debe de consultar al Servicio de Inmigración y Naturalización de los Estados Unidos o a un abogado de inmigración.

Introduction

The aim of this book is to help you to help yourself through the entire process of becoming a United States Citizen. Because this is a complete self-help book, you can prepare for citizenship in the convenience and comfort of home, at your leisure, and at your own pace. Samples of forms used along the way have been included to guide you.

The naturalization process, beginning with making application and ending with the hearing where you take your oath of allegiance, can take as little as a few months or as long as nearly two years. A wait of about one year is not uncommon. Most of this time, the application is out of your hands and is being processed by federal officials. So it is best to begin immediately, as soon as you are qualified. The sooner you start, the sooner you become a citizen.

Note

This book is intended to provide accurate and authoritative information regarding the process of naturalization for United States Citizenship. Every care has been taken in the writing of it, and appropriate individuals and reference materials have been consulted, especially those from the Immigration and Naturalization Service of the United States Department of Justice. However, federal laws regarding naturalization are subject to change. Therefore, for more detailed or updated information, particularly in complex cases, the applicant should consult the Immigration and Naturalization Service or an immigration attorney.

Capítulo 1
TODO LO REFERENTE A LA
NATURALIZACION

¿Que es la naturalización?

Sencillamente, "naturalización" quiere decir el hecho de que un extranjero se haga ciudadano. El Congreso ha aprobado leyes de naturalización que exponen las condiciones para que los inmigrantes se puedan hacer ciudadanos. Tales leyes intentan que un inmigrante pueda hacerse ciudadano solamente si el, o ella, está dispuesto a aceptar los deberes y las responsabilidades de ciudadanía y de conservar y proteger la democracia Americana. Las leyes son iguales para los hombres y las mujeres de toda raza. Todos se vuelven ciudadanos al seguir el mismo procedimiento. Este libro es para que usted se guíe par sí mismo por todo ese procedimiento.

¿Cuáles son los beneficios?

¿Por qué debe hacerse uno ciudadano de los Estados Unidos? Sin duda, usted tiene sus buenas razones personales que lo hacen querer ser un ciudadano de los Estados Unidos. Pero, cualesquiera que sean, además de tener ud. sus razones personales, es buen idea darse cuenta de los muchos e importantes beneficios de la naturalización, o ciudadanía estadounidense:
- Ud. va a poder votar en todas las elecciones.
- Ud. calificará para los trabajos que requieren la ciudadanía estadounidense.
- Ud. les facilitará a sus parientes cercanos que viven en el extranjero el que puedan inmigrar.
- Ud. ya no tendrá que cargar con su "mica" ni tendrá que notificarle al Servicio de Inmigración y Naturalización de su dirección.
- Ud. podrá obtener pasaporte que indica que es ciudadano de los Estates Unidos y posiblemente podrá viajar con más facilidad.El pasaporte de los Estados Unidos se considera, muchas veces, ser el más deseable.

Chapter 1
ALL ABOUT NATURALIZATION

What is naturalization?

Simply, "naturalization" means the becoming of a United States citizen by an alien. Congress has passed naturalization laws that set forth the conditions under which immigrants can become citizens. Such laws intend that an immigrant may become a citizen only if he or she is willing to accept the duties and responsibilities of citizenship and to preserve and protect American democracy. The laws are the same for men and women of all races. All become citizens by following the same procedure. This book is intended to guide you through those procedures, on your own.

What are the benefits of naturalization?

Why become a United States citizen? You undoubtedly have some good personal reasons prompting your desire to become a citizen of the United States. But in addition to your personal reasons, whatever they may be, it is a good idea to be aware of the many important benefits of naturalization, or United States citizenship:

- You will be able to vote in all elections.
- You will qualify for jobs that require United States citizenship.
- You will make immigration to the United States easier for your immediate relatives still abroad.
- You will no longer have to carry your alien registration card or notify the Immigration and Naturalization Service of your address.
- You will be able to obtain a passport indicating your United States citizenship, possibly making travel easier. A United States passport is often considered the most desirable to have.

•Ud. hasta podrá postularse para un puesto público con excepción a la presidencia o vice-presidencia de los Estados Unidos.

Es agradable saber que como ciudadano. ud. tambien puede compartir totalmente las libertades del país con todos los beneficios y las responsabilidades que representa la ciudadanía.

¿Quién se puede naturalizar?

Las personas como usted. Los extranjeros que inmigran legalmente a los Estados Unidos, que deciden hacerse ciudadanos, y que pasan por el procedimiento de la naturalización. Entonces pueden disfrutar de los beneficios completos de la ciudadanía Americana junto con todos los ciudadanos que nacieron en los Estados Unidos.

Muchos millones de personas antes que usted de todas partes del mundo, de todas las nacionalidades, creencias y colores han venido a los Estados Unidos a vivir. Debido a esto, no es extraño que se haya creado la expresión del "crisol". América...el crisol! Las razones personales de esta multitud que vino a radicar a los Estados Unidos y que se hicieron ciudadanos probablenente fueron tan variadas como las personas mismas. Sólo podemos suponer que todo inmigrante espera mejorar su vida al venir a vivir en los Estados Unidos – conocidos extensamente como la "tierra de la oportunidad".

Antes de comenzar el procedimiento de la solicitud, es importante asegurar que usted reúne los requisitos que lo hacen elegible para solicitar.

¿Cuáles son los requisitos para naturalizarse?

Antes de solicitar la naturalización, verifique el que usted reúna todo los ocho requisitos generales que siguen:

1. Debe de tener al menos 18 años de edad.

2. Debe de haber sido admitido legalmente a los Estados Unidos con residencia permanente.

• You can even run for public office, except that of President or Vice-President of the United States.

It is a nice feeling to know that as a citizen you, too, can fully share in this country's freedoms, with all the benefits and responsibilities that citizenship entails.

Who becomes naturalized?

People like yourself. Aliens who legally immigrate to the United States, who choose to become citizens, and who go through the naturalization process. Then they may enjoy the full benefits of citizenship right along with those citizens who were born in the United States.

Many millions of people before you, from all over the world, of all nationalities, creeds and colors have come to the United States to live. Because of this, it is no wonder that the expression "melting pot" evolved. America, the melting pot! The personal reasons for these multitudes settling in the United States and becoming citizens were probably as varied as the people themselves. We can only assume that all immigrants hope to better their lives by living in the United States — widely known as the "land of opportunity."

Before beginning the application process, it is important to make sure that you meet the requirements making you eligible to apply.

The requirements for naturalization

Before you apply for naturalization, check to see that you meet all eight of the following general requirements:

1. You must be at least 18 years old.

2. You must have been lawfully admitted into the United States for permanent residence.

3. Debe de haber vivido en los Estados Unidos constantemente por un mínimo de 5 años, sin contar viajes cortos afuera de los E.U.A. para ser elegible a solicitar la ciudadanía. También debe de haber vivido por três meses en el Estado o distritodel INS adonde inicia su petición.

Hay algunas excepciones importantes a este requisito de residencia. Una excepción es el estar casado con un(a) esposo (a) ciudadano(a); ésto puede cortar el requisito de residencia a 3 años. Otras excepciones se hacen para ciertos (as) esposos(as) de ciudadanos(as) empleados(as) en el extranjero y para los extranjeros miembros de las fuerzas armadas de los Estados Unidos. Véase el Apéndice 1, "Las Excepciones Para Residencia y Los Requisitos de Presencia Física" para los detalles sobre estas excepciones y también los reglamentos sobre las vacaciones. Ejemplares de los formularios N-470 y N-426 aparecen en el Apéndice 1 también. Son usadas por ciertos individuos en casos especiales para llenar los requisitos de residencia. Todavía otras excepciones al requisito de una residencia de 5 años se aplican a ciertos grupos de refugiados bajo lo que se llama la provisión "rollback". Para conocer más sobre esto, véase el Apéndice 2, "La Provisión "Rollback" y los Requisitos de Residencia".

4. Debe de mostrar una reputación honrada y debe creer en los principios de la Constitución de los Estados Unidos. Véase el Apéndice 3, "Reputación y Lealtad" para lo específico sobre éste requisito.

5. Debe de no haber pertenecido al partido Comunista por diez años antes de iniciar su solicitud, "La Petición para Naturalización".

6. No debe haber violado cualquier ley de inmigración ni de haber recibido una orden para salir de los E.U.

7. Debe poder hablar, comprender, leer y escribir un inglés sencillo, y tiene que pasar un examen sobre la historia y el gobierno de los Estados Unidos.

3. You must have lived in the United States continuously for at least 5 years, not counting short trips outside the U.S.A. Also, you must have resided for three months in the state or INS district where you file your petition.

   There are some important exceptions to this residency requirement. One exception is marriage to a citizen spouse, which can shorten the residency requirement to 3 years. Other exceptions are made for certain spouses of citizens employed abroad and for alien members of the United States armed forces. See Appendix 1, "Exceptions to Residence and Physical Presence Requirements" for details about these exceptions and also regulations about vacations. Samples of Forms N-470 and N-426 appear in Appendix 1, too. They are used by individuals in special cases to meet residency requirements. Still other exceptions to the 5 year residency requirement apply to certain refugee groups under what is called the "rollback" provision. For more on this, see Appendix 2, "The 'Rollback' Provision and Residency Requirements."

4. You must show good moral character and believe in the principles of the Constitution of the United States. See Appendix 3, "Character and Loyalty" for specifics on this requirement.

5. You must not have been a member of the Communist Party for ten years prior to filing your application, "Petition for Naturalization."

6. You must not have broken any immigration laws or have been ordered to leave the United States.

7. You must be able to speak, understand, read, and write simple English, and you must pass an examination about the history and government of the United States.

8. Debe de haber tomado el juramento prometiendo renunciar a fidelidad extranjera, obedecer la Constitución y las leyes de los Estado Unidos, y pelear por los E.U.A. o hacer trabajo que sea importante a la nación si se le pide hacerlo.

Luego que usted llene estos 8 requisitos generales, estará listo para comenzar los primeros tres pasos en el procedimiento de naturalización. Así es que seguimos al Capítulo 2, La Solicitud, que es su primer paso hacia la ciudadanía de los Estados Unidos.

8. You must take an oath promising to give up your foreign allegiance, to obey the Constitution and laws of the United States, and to fight for the U.S.A. or do work of importance to the nation, if asked to do so.

Once you think you meet these eight general requirements, you are ready to begin the first three steps in the naturalization process. So, onward to Chapter 2, The Application, which is your first step to United States citizenship.

THE TIDES OF LEGAL IMMIGRATION

People admitted legally in the last 50 years

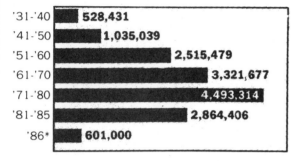

'31-'40	528,431
'41-'50	1,035,039
'51-'60	2,515,479
'61-'70	3,321,677
'71-'80	4,493,314
'81-'85	2,864,406
'86*	601,000

- Total number admitted 1820-1985: 52,527,650
- Projected admissions for 1986: 601,000
- Total projected 1820-1986: 53,128,650
- No. of foreigners now waiting to enter the U.S. legally: 1,903,475[1]

*Estimate.

[1]As of Jan. 1986. The estimated number waiting as of Jan. 1987 is 2,036,718.

Numbers waiting to enter U.S. by INS preference order

As of January 1986

First Preference (Unmarried children of U.S. citizens)	**11,764**
Second Preference (Spouses and unmarried children of legal aliens)	**346,728**
Third Preference (Professionals and exceptionally talented scientists and artists)	**28,460**
Fourth Preference (Married children of citizens)	**95,851**
Fifth Preference (Brothers and sisters of citizens)	**1,210,656**
Sixth Preference (Skilled and unskilled workers)	**48,740**
Non-Preference Category	**161,276**

Countries with largest number waiting to legally emigrate to U.S.

As of January 1986

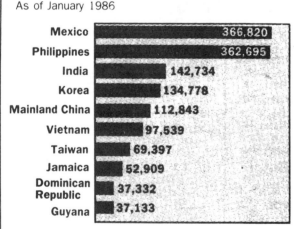

Mexico	366,820
Philippines	362,695
India	142,734
Korea	134,778
Mainland China	112,843
Vietnam	97,539
Taiwan	69,397
Jamaica	52,909
Dominican Republic	37,332
Guyana	37,133

How long it takes to immigrate legally

The wait for the highest preference immigrant — such as the spouses or unmarried children of U.S. citizens — would be a couple of months versus 25 to 30 years for some people trying to come in under the third preference category (members of professions or persons of exceptional scientific or artistic ability) from the Philippines.

SHORTEST
- First & fourth preference for a majority of countries: 2-3 months

LONGEST
- Third preference for Philippines: 16½ years
- Fifth preference for Hong Kong: 12 years, eight months
- Fifth preference for Philippines: 11 years, four months
- Fifth preference for Mexico: 10 years, 2½ months

SOURCE: U.S. Census Bureau & U.S. Immigration & Naturalization Service

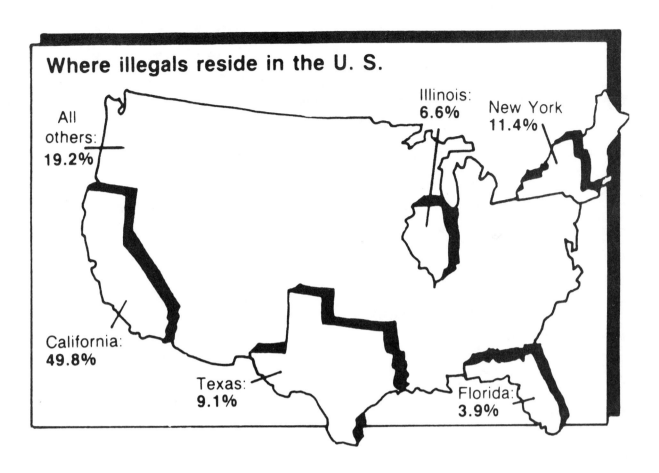

Where illegals reside in the U. S.

All others: **19.2%**

Illinois: **6.6%**

New York **11.4%**

California: **49.8%**

Texas: **9.1%**

Florida: **3.9%**

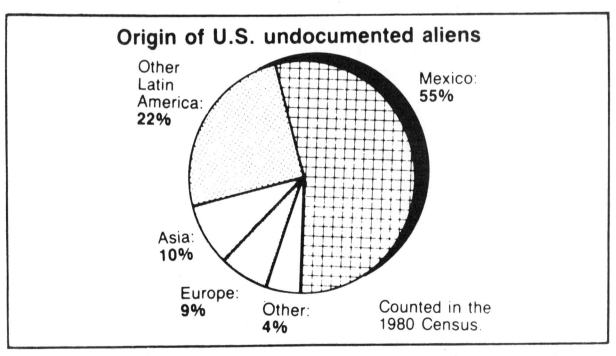

Origin of U.S. undocumented aliens

Other Latin America: **22%**

Mexico: **55%**

Asia: **10%**

Europe: **9%**

Other: **4%**

Counted in the 1980 Census.

Capítulo 2
LA SOLICITUD

El proceso entero de naturalización se cumple en tres pasos separados, el primero el cual es que usted complete su solicitud. Esto se hace solamente despues de llenar los 8 requisitos generales que se anotan en el capítulo 1.

Cuál solicitud se debe usar

La "Solicitud para Iniciar la Petición para Naturalización", el Formulario N-400, es el que usted usa si está solicitando su propia naturalización. El INS revisa este formulario de vez en cuando. Mientras que el INS acepta las formas más 'viejas,' valdría la pena obtener la más nueva. Las instrucciones en este libro vienen de la ultima revisión fechada 10/26/89. Mire usted la esquina al pie izquierdo de sus páginas del N-400 donde dice: Forma N-400 (10/26/89)N.

Su solicitud consiste de tres cosas:
1. La solicitud, Forma N-400, de cuatro páginas con instrucciones.
2. Una Carta de huellas digitales.
3. La Forma G-325, "Informe Biográfico", una hoja que viene con su carbón para tener una copia en duplicado. (G-325B tambien se usa si el servicio militar previo es parte del antecedente del solicitante. Si es que usted basa su solicitud sobre su servicio militar, tiene usted que presentar la Forma N-426, "Petición para la Certificación de Servicio Naval o Militar.")

El ejemplar 1, en éste capítulo, enseña los formularios N-400 y G-325 llenados, y se habla de una Carta de huellas digitales después de eso. El N-400 es la solicitud básica, la que más seguido se entrega al Servicio de Inmigración Y Naturalización (INS). Ya que se supone que los lectores de este libro estarán usando el N-400, éste es el enfoque de nuestra atención.

Chapter 2
THE APPLICATION

The entire naturalization process is accomplished in three separate steps, the first of which is for you to complete your application. This is done only after meeting the eight general requirements listed in Chapter 1.

Which application to use

The "Application to File Petition for Naturalization," Form N-400, is the one you use if you are applying for your own naturalization. The INS revises this form periodically. While they will accept the older application forms, it might be worth your while to obtain the latest one. The instructions in this book are for the latest revision dated 10/26/89. Look in the lower left corner of the pages of your N-400 where it should read: Form N-400 (10/26/89)N.

Your application consists of three items:
1. The application, Form N-400, which is four pages, plus instructions.
2. A fingerprint chart.
3. Form G-325, "Biographic Information," a sheet that comes with carbon paper for a duplicate copy. (G-325B is also to be used if previous military service is a part of the applicant's background. And, if your application is based on your military service, you must submit form N-426, "Request for Certification of Military or Naval Service.")

Sample 1, in this chapter, shows Forms N-400 and G-325 filled out, and the fingerprint chart is discussed after that. The N-400 is the basic application, the one most often submitted to the Immigration and Naturalization Service (INS). Since it is presumed that readers of this book will be using the N-400, it is the focus of attention.

Incluyendo A Los Hijos Menores

Si usted tiene hijos menores, debería de ponerlos a cada uno en la sección No. 26 de/la página 2 de su N-400.

Lo que sigue sólo se refiere a los solicitantes para naturalización que tengan hijos menores de 18 años de edad y nacidos en el extranjero.

Algunos de sus hijos (no hijastros) nacidos en el extranjero que todavía no sean ciudadanos posiblemente se vuelvan ciudadanos automáticamente cuando usted se naturalice. Esto sucede:

1. Si el niño es residente permanente legal de los Estados Unidos y tiene menos de 18 años de edad cuando usted se naturalice, y

2. Si el otro de los padres del niño ya es ciudadano o se hace ciudadano antes o al mismo tiempo que usted. Pero si el otro de los padres ya falleció o si ud. es divorciado o separado y tiene la custodia legal del niño, entonces no importa que el padre haya sido o no extranjero.

3. Si los padres del niño nunca se casaron y ud. es la madre, solo se aplica el artículo 1 anterior.

4. Si los padres del niño nunca se casaron y usted es el padre natural, el articulo 1 anterior se le aplica. Tiene que establecer que en la fecha del nacimiento del niño usted ya era ciudadano de los Estados Unidos; tiene que presentar una declaración notarizada de mantenimiento válida hasta que cumpla el niño sus 18 años; y tiene usted que reconocer su paternidad por escrito bajo juramento o tener una orden de Corte que declare que el niño es suya.

5. Si su niño es adoptado, está bajo su custodia, se le completó su adopción antes del decimo-sexto cumpleaños y es residente legal de los Estados Unidos.

Including minor children

If you have minor children, be sure to list each one in section #26 on page 2 of your N-400.

The following applies only to applicants for naturalization who have foreign-born children under 18 years of age.

Some or all of your foreign-born children (not step-children) who are not yet citizens may possibly become United States citizens automatically when you are naturalized. This will happen:

1. If the child is a lawful permanent resident of the United States and still under 18 years of age when you are naturalized, and

2. If the child's other parent is already a citizen or becomes a citizen before or at the same time that you become naturalized. If, however, the child's other parent is deceased, or if you are divorced or separated and have legal custody of the child, then it makes no difference that the child's other parent was or is an alien.

3. If the child's parents were never married and you are the mother, only Item 1. above applies.

4. If the child's parents were never married and you are the natural father, Item 1. above applies. However, you must establish that you were a United States citizen on the date of the child's birth; you must file an affidavit of support valid until the child's 18th birthday; and you must acknowledge paternity in writing under oath, or have a court order stating that the child is yours.

5. If your child is adopted, is in your custody, the adoption was completed before the child's 16th birthday, and if the child is a lawful resident of the United States.

Sample 1 – Form N-400
Application to File Petition for Naturalization

U.S. Department of Justice
Immigration and Naturalization Service

OMB #1115-0009
Application for Naturalization

START HERE - Please Type or Print

FOR INS USE ONLY

Part 1. Information about you.

Family Name: Garcia-Gonzalez
Given Name: Pedro
Middle Initial:

U.S. Mailing Address - Care of
Pedro Garcia-Gonzalez

Street Number and Name: 621 E. Emmett St.
Apt. #:

City: Santa Ana
County: Orange

State: California
ZIP Code: 92707

Date of Birth (month/day/year): December 3, 1948
Country of Birth: Mexico

Social Security #: 386-40-2563
A #: A-55 416 038

FOR INS USE ONLY
Returned
Receipt

Resubmitted

Reloc Sent

Reloc Rec'd

☐ Applicant Interviewed

Part 2. Basis for Eligibility (check one).

a. ☒ I have been a permanent resident for at least five (5) years .

b. ☐ I have been a permanent resident for at least three (3) years and have been married to a United States Citizen for those three years.

c. ☐ I am a permanent resident child of United States citizen parent(s) .

d. ☐ I am applying on the basis of qualifying military service in the Armed Forces of the U.S. and have attached completed Forms N-426 and G-325B

e. ☐ Other. (Please specify section of law) _____ .

At interview
☐ request naturalization ceremony at court

Remarks

Part 3. Additional information about you.

Date you became a permanent resident (month/day/year): March 14, 1971
Port admitted with an immmigrant visa or INS Office where granted adjustment of status.: San Ysidro, California

Citizenship: Mexico

Name on alien registration card (if different than in Part 1): Same

Other names used since you became a permanent resident (including maiden name): None

Sex: ☒ Male ☐ Female
Height: 5' 11"
Marital Status: ☐ Single ☒ Married ☐ Divorced ☐ Widowed

Can you speak, read and write English ? ☐No ☒Yes.

Absences from the U.S.:

Have you been absent from the U.S. since becoming a permanent resident? ☒ No ☐Yes.

If you answered **"Yes"** , complete the following, Begin with your most recent absence. If you need more room to explain the reason for an absence or to list more trips, continue on separate paper.

Action

Date left U.S.	Date returned	Did absence last 6 months or more?	Destination	Reason for trip
not applicable		☐ Yes ☐ No		
		☐ Yes ☐ No		
		☐ Yes ☐ No		
		☐ Yes ☐ No		
		☐ Yes ☐ No		
		☐ Yes ☐ No		

To Be Completed by Attorney or Representative, if any
☐ Fill in box if G-28 is attached to represent the applicant

VOLAG#

ATTY State License #

Form N-400 (Rev. 07/17/91)N
Continued on back.

Part 4. Information about your residences and employment.

A. List your addresses during the last five (5) years or since you became a permanent resident, whichever is less. Begin with your current address. If you need more space, continue on separate paper:

Street Number and Name, City, State, Country, and Zip Code	Dates (month/day/year)	
	From	To
621 E. Emmett St., Santa Ana, CA 92707	2/1/86	present

B. List your employers during the last five (5) years. List your present or most recent employer first. If none, write "None". If you need more space, continue on separate paper.

Employer's Name	Employer's Address	Dates Employed (month/day/year)		Occupation/position
	Street Name and Number - City, State and ZIP Code	From	To	
Fairway Landscape	991 Manitoba Corona, CA 91720	1/10/86	present	Gardener

Part 5. Information about your marital history.

A. Total number of times you have been married ___1___ . If you are now married, complete the following regarding your husband or wife.

Family name	Given name	Middle initial
Garcia-Gonzalez	Laura	none

Address
621 E. Emmett St., Santa Ana, CA 92707

Date of birth (month/day/year) October 10, 1954	Country of birth Mexico	Citizenship Mexico

Social Security# 320-56-8717	A# (if applicable) A13 691 385	Immigration status (If not a U.S. citizen) Alien

Naturalization (If applicable)
(month/day/year) not applicable   Place   (City, State)

If you have ever previously been married or if your current spouse has been previously married, please provide the following on separate paper: Name of prior spouse, date of marriage, date marriage ended, how marriage ended and immigration status of prior spouse.

Part 6. Information about your children.

B. Total Number of Children ___1___   Complete the following information for each of your children. If the child lives with you, state "with me" in the address column; otherwise give city/state/country of child's current residence. If deceased, write "deceased" in the address column.   If you need more space, continue on separate paper.

Full name of child	Date of birth	Country of birth	Citizenship	A - Number	Address
Jose Garcia-Gonzalez	1/3/89	Mexico	Mexico	A13-691-386	621 E. Emmett St. Santa Ana, CA 92707

Form N-400 (Rev 07/17/91)N   **Continued on next page**

Continued on back

Part 7. Additional eligibility factors.

Please answer each of the following questions. If your answer is **"Yes"**, explain on a separate paper.

1. Are you now, or have you ever been a member of, or in any way connected or associated with the Communist Party, or ever knowingly aided or supported the Communist Party directly, or indirectly through another organization, group or person, or ever advocated, taught, believed in, or knowingly supported or furthered the interests of communism? ☐ Yes ☒ No
2. During the period March 23, 1933 to May 8, 1945, did you serve in, or were you in any way affiliated with, either directly or indirectly, any military unit, paramilitary unit, police unit, self-defense unit, vigilante unit, citizen unit of the Nazi party or SS, government agency or office, extermination camp, concentration camp, prisoner of war camp, prison, labor camp, detention camp or transit camp, under the control or affiliated with:
    a. The Nazi Government of Germany? ☐ Yes ☒ No
    b. Any government in any area occupied by, allied with, or established with the assistance or cooperation of, the Nazi Government of Germany? ☐ Yes ☒ No
3. Have you at any time, anywhere, ever ordered, incited, assisted, or otherwise participated in the persecution of any person because of race, religion, national origin, or political opinion? ☐ Yes ☒ No
4. Have you ever left the United States to avoid being drafted into the U.S. Armed Forces? ☐ Yes ☒ No
5. Have you ever failed to comply with Selective Service laws? ☐ Yes ☒ No
    If you have registered under the Selective Service laws, complete the following information:
    Selective Service Number:_____ Date Registered:_____
    If you registered before 1978, also provide the following:
    Local Board Number:_____ Classification:_____
6. Did you ever apply for exemption from military service because of alienage, conscientious objections or other reasons? ☐ Yes ☒ No
7. Have you ever deserted from the military, air or naval forces of the United States? ☐ Yes ☒ No
8. Since becoming a permanent resident, have you ever failed to file a federal income tax return? ☐ Yes ☒ No
9. Since becoming a permanent resident, have you filed a federal income tax return as a nonresident or failed to file a federal return because you considered yourself to be a nonresident? ☐ Yes ☒ No
10 Are deportation proceedings pending against you, or have you ever been deported, or ordered deported, or have you ever applied for suspension of deportation? ☐ Yes ☒ No
11. Have you ever claimed in writing, or in any way, to be a United States citizen? ☐ Yes ☒ No
12. Have you ever:
    a. been a habitual drunkard? ☐ Yes ☒ No
    b. advocated or practiced polygamy? ☐ Yes ☒ No
    c. been a prostitute or procured anyone for prostitution? ☐ Yes ☒ No
    d. knowingly and for gain helped any alien to enter the U.S. illegally? ☐ Yes ☒ No
    e. been an illicit trafficker in narcotic drugs or marijuana? ☐ Yes ☒ No
    f. received income from illegal gambling? ☐ Yes ☒ No
    g. given false testimony for the purpose of obtaining any immigration benefit? ☐ Yes ☒ No
13. Have you ever been declared legally incompetent or have you ever been confined as a patient in a mental institution? ☐ Yes ☒ No
14. Were you born with, or have you acquired in same way, any title or order of nobility in any foreign State? ☐ Yes ☒ No
15. Have you ever:
    a. knowingly committed any crime for which you have not been arrested? ☐ Yes ☒ No
    b. been arrested, cited, charged, indicted, convicted, fined or imprisoned for breaking or violating any law or ordinance excluding traffic regulations? ☐ Yes ☒ No

(If you answer yes to 15 , in your explanation give the following information for each incident or occurrence the **city**, **state**, and **country**, where the offense took place, the **date** and **nature** of the offense, and the **outcome** or **disposition** of the case).

Part 8. Allegiance to the U.S.

If your answer to any of the following questions is **"NO"**, attach a full explanation:
1. Do you believe in the Constitution and form of government of the U.S.? ☒ Yes ☐ No
2. Are you willing to take the full Oath of Allegiance to the U.S.? (see instructions) ☒ Yes ☐ No
3. If the law requires it, are you willing to bear arms on behalf of the U.S.? ☒ Yes ☐ No
4. If the law requires it, are you willing to perform noncombatant services in the Armed Forces of the U.S.? ☒ Yes ☐ No
5. If the law requires it, are you willing to perform work of national importance under civilian direction? ☒ Yes ☐ No

Form N-400 (Rev 07/17/91)N

Continued on back

Part 9. Memberships and organizations.

A. List your present and past membership in or affiliation with every organization, association, fund, foundation, party, club, society, or similar group in the United States or in any other place. Include any military service in this part. If none, write "none". Include the name of organization, location, dates of membership and the nature of the organization. If additional space is needed, use separate paper.

None

Part 10. Complete only if you checked block " C " in Part 2.

How many of your parents are U.S. citizens? ☐ One ☐ Both (Give the following about one U.S. citizen parent:)

Family Name	Given Name	Middle Name

Address

Basis for citizenship:
☐ Birth
☐ Naturalization Cert. No.

Relationship to you (check one): ☐ natural parent ☐ adoptive parent
☐ parent of child legitimated after birth

If adopted or legitimated after birth, give date of adoption or, legitimation: *(month/day/year)*_____

Does this parent have legal custody of you? ☐ Yes ☐ No

(Attach a copy of relating evidence to establish that you are the child of this U.S. citizen and evidence of this parent's citizenship.)

Part 11. Signature. *(Read the information on penalties in the instructions before completing this section).*

I certify or, if outside the United States, I swear or affirm, under penalty of perjury under the laws of the United States of America that this application, and the evidence submitted with it, is all true and correct. I authorize the release of any information from my records which the Immigration and Naturalization Service needs to determine eligibility for the benefit I am seeking.

Signature	Date
Pedro Garcia-Gonzalez	8/2/91

Please Note: If you do not completely fill out this form, or fail to submit required documents listed in the instructions, you may not be found eligible for naturalization and this application may be denied.

Part 12. Signature of person preparing form if other than above. *(Sign below)*

I declare that I prepared this application at the request of the above person and it is based on all information of which I have knowledge.

Signature	Print Your Name	Date

Firm Name
and Address

DO NOT COMPLETE THE FOLLOWING UNTIL INSTRUCTED TO DO SO AT THE INTERVIEW

I swear that I know the contents of this application, and supplemental pages 1 through_____, that the corrections , numbered 1 through_____, were made at my request, and that this amended application, is true to the best of my knowledge and belief.

_____
(Complete and true signature of applicant)

Subscribed and sworn to before me by the applicant.

_____
(Examiner's Signature)   Date

Sample 2 – Form G-325
Biographic Information

U.S. Department of Justice

Immigration and Naturalization Service

BIOGRAPHIC INFORMATION

OMB No. 1115-0066

(Family name)	(First name)	(Middle name)	
GARCIA-GONZALEZ	Pedro		

☒ MALE ☐ FEMALE | BIRTHDATE (Mo.-Day-Yr.) 12/03/48 | NATIONALITY Mexican | FILE NUMBER A55 416 038

ALL OTHER NAMES USED (Including names by previous marriages)
none

CITY AND COUNTRY OF BIRTH
San Pulco, Mexico

SOCIAL SECURITY NO. (If any) 386402563

	FAMILY NAME	FIRST NAME	DATE, CITY AND COUNTRY OF BIRTH (If known)	CITY AND COUNTRY OF RESIDENCE.
FATHER	Garcia,	Roberto	1/12/28 San Pulco, Mexico	Deceased
MOTHER (Maiden name)	Gonzalez, Maria		12/03/29 San Pulco, Mexico	San Pulco, Mexico

HUSBAND (If none, so state) OR WIFE	FAMILY NAME (For wife, give maiden name)	FIRST NAME	BIRTHDATE	CITY & COUNTRY OF BIRTH	DATE OF MARRIAGE	PLACE OF MARRIAGE
	Sanchez	Laura	10/10/54	Ensenada, Mexico	1/26/88	Corona, CA USA

FORMER HUSBANDS OR WIVES (If none, so state)

FAMILY NAME (For wife, give maiden name)	FIRST NAME	BIRTHDATE	DATE & PLACE OF MARRIAGE	DATE AND PLACE OF TERMINATION OF MARRIAGE
none				

APPLICANT'S RESIDENCE LAST FIVE YEARS. LIST PRESENT ADDRESS FIRST.

STREET AND NUMBER	CITY	PROVINCE OR STATE	COUNTRY	FROM MONTH	YEAR	TO MONTH	YEAR
621 E. Emmett St.	Santa Ana, California		USA	Feb.	1986	PRESENT TIME	

APPLICANT'S LAST ADDRESS OUTSIDE THE UNITED STATES OF MORE THAN ONE YEAR

STREET AND NUMBER	CITY	PROVINCE OR STATE	COUNTRY	FROM MONTH	YEAR	TO MONTH	YEAR
222 Aquiles Serdan	San Pulco	Zacatecas	Mexico	Dec.	1948	Feb.	1971

APPLICANT'S EMPLOYMENT LAST FIVE YEARS. (IF NONE, SO STATE) LIST PRESENT EMPLOYMENT FIRST

FULL NAME AND ADDRESS OF EMPLOYER	OCCUPATION (SPECIFY)	FROM MONTH	YEAR	TO MONTH	YEAR
Fairway Landscape Inc., 991 Manitoba, Corona, CA	Gardener	Jan.	1986	PRESENT TIME	

Show below last occupation abroad if not shown above. (Include all information requested above.)

Self-employed, San Pulco, Mexico - Farmer		Dec.	1967	Feb.	1971

THIS FORM IS SUBMITTED IN CONNECTION WITH APPLICATION FOR:

☒ NATURALIZATION ☐ OTHER (SPECIFY):
☐ STATUS AS PERMANENT RESIDENT

SIGNATURE OF APPLICANT
Pedro Garcia-Gonzalez

DATE

IF YOUR NATIVE ALPHABET IS IN OTHER THAN ROMAN LETTERS, WRITE YOUR NAME IN YOUR NATIVE ALPHABET IN THIS SPACE

Are all copies legible? ☒ Yes

PENALTIES: SEVERE PENALTIES ARE PROVIDED BY LAW FOR KNOWINGLY AND WILLFULLY FALSIFYING OR CONCEALING A MATERIAL FACT.

APPLICANT: BE SURE TO PUT YOUR NAME AND ALIEN REGISTRATION NUMBER IN THE BOX OUTLINED BY HEAVY BORDER BELOW.

COMPLETE THIS BOX (Family name)	(Given name)	(Middle name)	(Alien registration number)
GARCIA-GONZALEZ, Pedro			A55 416 038

Form G-325 (Rev. 10-1-82) Y

(1) Ident.

Si quiere, puede usted solicitar un certificado de ciudadanía para sus hijos sobre la Forma N-600, "Solicitud para el Certificado de Ciudadanía", con su pruebe de su propia naturalización.

Solicitudes Para Clases Especiales

Hay otras solicitudes para clases especiales de personas, tal como el Formulario N-402, "Solicitud para Iniciar Peticiones de Naturalización a Nombre de un Niño" y el Formulario N-600, "Solicitud para Certificado de Ciudadanía". Ya que el N-400 es el que usted estará usando con más probabilidad, sigue sólo una breve descripción y copias ejemplares de dos solicitudes.

El Formulario N-402 es la solicitud que se usará para la naturalización de niños que no se vuelven automáticamente ciudadanos a través de sus padres. Por ejemplo, si sólo uno de los padres del niño se naturaliza y el otro permanece como residente, el niño no se vuelve automáticamente ciudadano. El padre ciudadano de un niño extranjero tiene que llenar el Formulario N-402; esto se puede hacer en cualquier momento despues que el padre se haga ciudadano. Junto con esta solicitud usted debe de entregar:

1. Un formulario de Información Biográfica, G-325,
2. Una Carta de huellas digitales (sólo si el niño tiene 14 años o más).
3. Tres fotografías tomadas dentro de los 30 días a partir de la fecha en la cual se entregó la solicitud.

El tiempo es muy importante porque todos los tres pasos del procedimiento de naturalización se deben de completar antes de que cumpla el niño 18 años. En otras palabras, el niño debe de ser admitido como ciudadano antes de que cumpla los 18 años. Ya que el procedimiento de naturalización puede tomar bastante más que un año, planee entregar el Formulario N-402 al menos cuando su niño tenga 16 años, y sería mejor si fuera antes, de ser posible.

El ejemplar 3 enseña el Formulario N-402, "Solicitud para Iniciar una Petición de Naturalización a Nombre de un Niño". Para más información referente a cuándo se debe de usar ésta solicitud, consulte el

If you wish, you may apply for a certificate of citizenship in the name of your child(ren) by filing Form N-600, "Application for Certificate of Citizenship." This will show that they became citizens on the same date the parent was naturalized.

Applications for special classes:

There are other applications for special classes of persons, such as Form N-402, "Application to File Petition for Naturalization in Behalf of Child" and Form N-600, "Application for Certificate of Citizenship." However, since the N-400 is the one you will most likely be using, only a brief description and sample copies of these other two applications follow.

Form N-402 is the application to be used for the naturalization of children who do not become citizens automatically through their parent(s). For example, if only one of the child's parents becomes naturalized and the other remains a permanent resident, the child does not automatically become a citizen. Instead, the citizen parent of an alien child must complete Form N-402, which can be done at any time after the parent becomes a citizen. Along with this application you must submit:

1. a G-325 Biographic Information form,
2. a fingerprint chart (only if the child is age 14 or older),
3. Three photographs taken within 30 days of the date the application is submitted.

Timing is very important here because all three steps of the naturalization process must be completed before the child's 18th birthday. In other words, the child must actually be admitted to citizenship prior to becoming age 18. Because the naturalization process can take well over a year, plan to submit Form N-402 at least by the time your child is age 16, or even sooner, if at all possible.

Sample 3 shows Form N-402, "Application to File Petition for Naturalization in Behalf of Child." For more information regarding when to use this application, consult the pamphlet **Form N-17**, "Naturalization Requirements and General Information," particularly the

Sample 3 – Form N-402
Application in Behalf of Child

U.S. Department of Justice Immigration and Naturalization Service	**Application to File Petition for** OMB 1115-0010 **Naturalization in Behalf of Child** Under Section 322 of the Immigration and Nationality Act

Take or Mail to:
Immigration and Naturalization Service

Child's Name and Alien Registration Number

Name   Raymond Francois RANIERE

No.   A 55 418 036

I (We), the undersigned, desire that a petition for naturalization be filed in behalf of my (our) child.

1) My full, true, and correct name is   (Full, true name of citizen parent or citizen adoptive parent, without abbbreviations)

    Thomas Raniere

2) My present place of residence is   (Apt. No.)   (Number and street)   (City or town)   (Country)   (State)   (ZIP Code)

    7751 Liberty Avenue   Huntington Beach   U.S.A.   CA   92647

3) I am a citizen of the United States of America and was born on   (Month/Day/Year)   In   (City/State/Country)

    1/2/49   Brooklyn, NY,   U.S.A.

(If not a native born citizen) I was naturalized on (Month/Day/Year)

    not applicable

Certificate No.   Or I became a citizen of the United States through

Is the child's other parent a citizen of the United States?

   ☐ Yes   ☐ No

Complete (1a) to (3a) only if second parent wishes to join in application.

1a) My full, true, and correct name is   (Full, true name of citizen parent or citizen adoptive parent, without abbbreviations)

    not applicable

2a) My present place of residence is   (Apt. No.)   (Number and street)   (City or town)   (Country)   (State)   (ZIP Code)

3a) I am a citizen of the United States of America and was born on   (Month/Day/Year)   In   (City/State/Country)

(If not a native born citizen) I was naturalized on (Month/Day/Year)   At   (City and State)

Certificate No.   Or, I became a citizen of the United States through

---

The following (4 to 19) must be answered by all applicants.

4) I am (we are) the parent(s) of (Full, true name of child, without abbreviations) in whose behalf this application for naturalization is filed.

    Raymond Francois Raniere

5) The said child now resides with me (us) at   (Apt. No.)   (Number and street)   (City or town)   (Counry)   (State)   (ZIP Code)

    7751 Liberty Avenue   Huntington Beach   U.S.A.   CA   92647

6) The said child was born on (Month/Day/Year);   In (City/Country)

    1/25/75   The Hague, Netherlands

and is a citizen, subject, or national of (Country)   and is

    Netherlands   ☒ Single   ☐ Married

7) The said child was lawfully admitted to the United States for permanent residence on (Month/Day/Year)   At (City/State)

    May 3, 1982   Los Angeles, CA

Under the name of;   and

    Raymond Francois Raniere   ☒ Does   ☐ Does not intend to reside permanently in the United States.

8) I (We) desire the naturalization court to change the name of the child to (Give full name desired, without abbreviations)

    not applicable

9) If application is in behalf of an adopted child: I (we) adopted said child on (Month/Day/Year)   At   (City) (State)

    January 3, 1980   The Hague, Netherlands

In the (Name of Court)   At   (City or town)   (State)   (Country)

    The Hague Court   The Hague   Netherlands

The said child has resided continuously in the United States with me (us) in my (our) legal custody since (Month/Day/Year)

    May 3, 1982

Form N-402 (10/31/89) N

10) Since such child's lawful admission to the United States for permanent residence, the child has not been absent from the United States at any time except as follows (If none, state "None")

Departed from the United States		Returned to the United States	
Port	Date (Month/Day/Year)	Port	Date (Month/Day/Year)
None			

11) Has such child ever been a patient in a mental institution, or ever been treated for a mental illness?
☐ Yes   ☒ No

12) The law provides that a person may not be regarded as qualified for naturalizaiton under certain conditions, if the person knowingly committed certain offenses or crimes, even though not arrested therefor. Has such child ever in or outside the United States:

a)   Knowingly committed any crime for which he/she has not been arrested?
☐ Yes   ☒ No

b)   Been arrested, charged with violation of any law or ordinance, summoned into court as a defendant, convicted, fined, imprisoned, or placed on probation or parole, or forfeited collateral for any act involving a crime, misdemeanor, or breach of any law or ordinancy?
☐ Yes   ☒ No

If the answer to a) or b) is "Yes." on a separate sheet, give the following information as to each incident: when and where occurred, offense involved, and outcome of case if any.

13) Are deportation proceedings pending against such child or has such child ever been deported or ordered deported, or has such child ever applied for suspension of deportation or for preexamination?
☐ Yes   ☒ No

14) List the child's membership in every organization, association, fund, foundation, party, club, society, or similar group in the United States and in any other place, during the past ten years, and his foreign military service. (If none, write "None.")
None   ☐ Yes   ☐ No

15) Has such child ever served in the Armed Forces of the United States?
☐ Yes   ☒ No

16) (Answer only if the child is of an understanding age.) If the law requires it, is the child willing to bear arms or perform noncombatant service in the Armed Forces of the United States or perform work of national importance under civilian directon? If "No" explain fully on a separate sheet of paper.
☒ Yes   ☐ No

17) Since the child's lawful admission to the United States for permanent residence, my wife (husband) and I have been absent from the United States as follows (if no absences, state "None"):

None

18) My wife (husband) and I have been married as follows (give informaton as to each marriage): (Use extra sheet of papaer if necessary.)

Date Married	Date Marriage Ended	Name of Spouse	How Marriage Ended (Death or divorce)
12/12/79	not applicable	Claire Weddik	not applicable

19) A petition for naturalization:
☒ Has not   ☐ has been filed on behalf of said child (if one has been filed, complete all of item 19)

Filed on (Month/Day/Year)   At (City/County/State)   In (Name of court)
not applicable

The present status of the previously filed petition is:
☐ Denied   ☐ Unknown   ☐ Other (explain)

Form N-402 (10/31/89) N

Thomas Raniere
(Signature of 1st parent)

7751 Liberty Ave., Huntington Beach,
(Address of 1st parent)   CA 92647

(714) 100-9990   March 7, 1989
(Telephone No.)   (Date)

Claire Weddik
(Signature of 2nd parent)

7751 Liberty Ave., Huntington Beach,
(Address of 2nd parent)   CA   92647

(714) 100-9900   March 7, 1989
(Telephone No.)   (Date)

SIGNATURE OF PERSON PREPARING FORM, IF OTHER THAN APPLICANT(S)

I declare that this document was prepared by me at the request of the applicant(s) and is based on all information of which I have any knowledge.

(Signature)   _(Address)_   _(Date)_

TO APPLICANTS: DO NOT WRITE BELOW THESE LINES

AFFIDAVIT

I do swear (affirm) that I know the contents of this application comprising pages 1 to 3, inclusive, subscribed by me; that the same are true to the best of my knowledge and belief; that correction(s) number(ed) (   ) to (   ) were made by me or at my request; and that this applicaton was signed by me with my full, true name.

_____
(Complete and true signature of 1st parent)

_____
(Complete and true signature of 2nd parent)

Subscribed and sworn   (affirmed) to before me at the preliminary investigation (examination) at

this _____ day of _____ , 19 ____

I certify that before verification the parent(s) stated in my presence that he (she/they) had read or heard the foregoing application and corrections therein and understood the contents thereof.

_____
(Naturalization Examiner)

Nonfiled _____

(Date, Reasons) _____

☆ U.S. GOVERNMENT PRINTING OFFICE: 1990 – 262–210 – 415/15184

Form N-402 (10/31/89) N

U.S. DEPARTMENT OF JUSTICE
IMMIGRATION AND NATURALIZATION SERVICE

APPLICATION FOR CERTIFICATE OF CITIZENSHIP

FEE STAMP

OMB No. 1115–0018
Approval Expires 7/31/85

Take or mail this application to:
IMMIGRATION AND NATURALIZATION SERVICE

Date __March 3, 1986__

(Print or type) __Maria Ulloa-Contreras__ ... nee __same__
(Full, True Name, without Abbreviations) .... (Maiden name, if any)
__1004 S. Standard__
(Apartment number, Street address, and, if appropriate, "in care of")
__Santa Ana,   Orange,   California   92701__
(City)   (County)   (State)   (ZIP Code)
__none__
(Telephone Number)

ALIEN REGISTRATION
No. __none__

(SEE INSTRUCTIONS. BE SURE YOU UNDERSTAND EACH QUESTION BEFORE YOU ANSWER IT.)

I hereby apply to the Commissioner of Immigration and Naturalization for a certificate showing that I am a citizen of the United States of America.

(1) I was born in __Mexicali,   Baja California__ on __4-11-62__
(City) .... (State or country) .... (Month) (Day) (Year)

(2) My personal description is: Sex __F__; complexion __dark__; color of eyes __black__; color of hair __black__;
height __5__ feet __3__ inches; weight __130__ pounds; visible distinctive marks __none__
Marital status: ☒ Single;   ☐ Married;   ☐ Divorced;   ☐ Widow(er).

(3) I arrived in the United States at __San Ysidro, California__ on __9-7-72__
(City and State) .... (Month) (Day) (Year)
under the name __Maria Ulloa-Contreras__ by means of __car__
(Name of ship or other means of arrival)

☐ on U.S. Passport No. __not applicable__ issued to me at .... on .... ;
(Month) (Day) (Year)
☐ on an Immigrant Visa. ☒ Other (specify) __birth certificate__

(4) FILL IN THIS BLOCK ONLY IF YOU ARRIVED IN THE UNITED STATES BEFORE JULY 1, 1924.
(a) My last permanent foreign residence was __not applicable__
(City) .... (Country)
(b) I took the ship or other conveyance to the United States at ....
(City) .... (Country)
(c) I was coming to ....
(Name of person in the United States) ... at .... (City and State where this person was living)
(d) I traveled to the United States with ....
(Names of passengers or relatives with whom you traveled, and their relationship to you, if any)

(5) Have you been out of the United States since you first arrived? ☐ Yes ☒ No. If "Yes" fill in the following information for every absence.

DATE DEPARTED	DATE RETURNED	NAME OF AIRLINE, OR OTHER MEANS USED TO RETURN TO THE UNITED STATES	PORT OF RETURN TO THE UNITED STATES

(6) I __have not__ filed a petition for naturalization.
(have) (have not)
(If "have", attach full explanation.)

TO THE APPLICANT.—Do not write between the double lines below.   Continue on next page.

ARRIVAL RECORDS EXAMINED	ARRIVAL RECORD FOUND
Card index	Place .... Date ....
Index books	Name ....
Manifests	
....	Manner ....
....	Marital status .... Age ....
....	(Signature of person making search)

Form N–600 (Rev. 5–5–83)N   (1)

(CONTINUE HERE)

(7) I claim United States citizenship through my (*check whichever applicable*) ☒ father; ☐ mother; ☐ both parents;

☐ adoptive parent(s)   ☐ husband

(8) My father's name is Roberto Ulloa ....; he was born on 5-16-30
                                                                                      (Month) (Day) (Year)

at ....Anaheim, California........U.S.A.; and resides at 551 River Rd. Corona, California
          (City)   (State or country)   (Street address, city, and State or country. If dead, write

He became a citizen of the United States by ☒ birth; ☐ naturalization on ....
"dead" and date of death.)   (Month) (Day) (Year)

in the ....not applicable................................ Certificate of Naturalization No. ....;
        (Name of court, city, and State)

☐ through his parent(s), and .... issued Certificate of Citizenship No. A or AA ....
                              (was)   (was not)

(If known) His former Alien Registration No. was ....

He has not lost United States citizenship. (*If citizenship lost, attach full explanation.*)
    (has) (has not)

He resided in the United States from 1930 to 1935 ; from 1950 to present from .... to ....;
                                     (Year) (Year)   (Year)   (Year)   (Year)   (Year)

from .... to ....; from .... to ....; I am the child of his ....1st........ marriage.
     (Year)   (Year)   (Year)   (Year)   (1st, 2d, 3d, etc.)

(9) My mother's present name is Carolina Contreras-Ulloa; her maiden name was Carolina Contreras-Espoza

she was born on 12-25-32 ....; at Guadalajara, Jalisco, Mexico ....; she resides
                (Month) (Day) (Year)   (City)   (State or country)

at 551 River Rd. Corona, California .... She became a citizen of the United States
   (Street address, city, and State or country. If dead, write "dead" and date of death.)

by ☐ birth; ☐ naturalization under the name of ..not applicable..

on .... in the ....
   (Month) (Day) (Year)   (Name of court, city, and State)

Certificate of Naturalization No. ....; ☐ through her parent(s), and .... issued Certificate
                                                                                       (was) (was not)

of Citizenship No. A or AA .... (If known) Her former Alien Registration No. was ....

She .... lost United States citizenship. (*If citizenship lost, attach full explanation.*)
    (has) (has not)

She resided in the United States from 1959 to present from .... to ....; from .... to ....; from ....
                                      (Year)   (Year)   (Year)   (Year)   (Year)   (Year)   (Year)

to ....; from .... to ....; I am the child of her ....1st........ marriage.
   (Year)   (Year)   (Year)   (1st, 2d, 3d, etc.)

(10) My mother and my father were married to each other on 6-14-58 at Mexicali, Baja Calif. Mexico
                                                           (Month) (Day) (Year) (City)   (State or country)

(11) If claim is through adoptive parent(s):
     I was adopted on ....not applicable.............. in the ....
                       (Month) (Day) (Year)   (Name of Court)

at .... by my ....
   (City or town) (State) (Country)   (mother, father, parents)

who were not United States citizens at that time.

(12) My .... served in the Armed Forces of the United States from ....
        (father) (mother)   (Date)

to .... and .... honorably discharged.
   (Date)   (was) (was not)

(13) I have not lost my United States citizenship. (*If citizenship lost, attach full explanation.*)
     (have) (have not)

(14) I submit the following documents with this application:

Nature of Document	Names of Persons Concerned
Birth Certificate	Applicant (Maria Ulloa-Contreras)
Marriage Certificate	Parents (Roberto & Carolina Ulloa)
Birth Certificate	Father (Roberto Ulloa)

(2)

38

(15) Fill in this block if your brother, sister, mother or father ever applied to the Immigration Service for a certificate of citizenship.

NAME OF RELATIVE	RELATIONSHIP	Date of Birth	WHEN APPLICATION SUBMITTED	CERTIFICATE No. AND FILE No., IF KNOWN, AND LOCATION OF OFFICE

(16) Fill in this block only if you are now or ever have been a married woman. I have been married .... time(s), as follows: (1, 2, 3, etc.)

			IF MARRIAGE HAS BEEN TERMINATED:	
DATE MARRIED	NAME OF HUSBAND	CITIZENSHIP OF HUSBAND	Date Marriage Ended	How Marriage Ended (Death or divorce)

(17) Fill in this block only if you claim citizenship through a husband. (*Marriage must have occurred prior to September 22, 1922.*)
Name of citizen husband ..not applicable......................; he was born on ....
(Give full and complete name)   (Month)   (Day)   (Year)
at ....; and resides at ....
        (City)   (State or country)   (Street address, city, and State or country. If dead, write
.... He became a citizen of the United States by ☐ birth; ☐ naturalization on ....
"dead" and date of death.)   (Month)   (Day)   (Year)
in the .... Certificate of Naturalization No. ....;
              (Name of court, city, and State)
☐ through his parent(s), and .... issued Certificate of Citizenship No. A or AA ....
                                          (was)   (was not)
He .... since lost United States citizenship. (*If citizenship lost, attach full explanation.*)
      (has)   (has not)
I am of the .... race. Before my marriage to him, he was married .... time(s), as follows:
                                                                                            (1, 2, 3, etc.)

		IF MARRIAGE HAS BEEN TERMINATED:	
DATE MARRIED	NAME OF WIFE	Date Marriage Ended	How Marriage Ended (Death or divorce)

(18) Fill in this block only if you claim citizenship through your stepfather. (*Applicable only if mother married U.S. Citizen prior to September 22, 1922.*)
The full name of my stepfather is ..not applicable...................; he was born on ....
                                                                                      (Month)   (Day)   (Year)
at ....; and resides at ....
        (City)   (State or country)   (Street address, city, and State or country. If dead, write
.... He became a citizen of the United States by ☐ birth; ☐ naturalization on ....
"dead" and date of death.)   (Month)   (Day)   (Year)
in the .... Certificate of Naturalization No. ....;
              (Name of court, city, and State)
☐ through his parent(s), and .... issued Certificate of Citizenship No. A or AA ....
                                          (was)   (was not)
He .... since lost United States citizenship. (*If citizenship lost, attach full explanation.*)
      (has)   (has not)
He and my mother were married to each other on ....at ....
                                                            (Month)   (Day)   (Year)   (City and State or country)
My mother is of the .... race. She .... issued Certificate of Citizenship No. A ....
                                                              (was)   (was not)
Before marrying my mother, my stepfather was married .... time(s), as follows:
                                                                              (1, 2, 3, etc.)

		IF MARRIAGE HAS BEEN TERMINATED:	
DATE MARRIED	NAME OF WIFE	Date Marriage Ended	How Marriage Ended (Death or divorce)

(19) I have ..not.... previously applied for a certificate of citizenship on ...., at ....
      (have)   (have not)   (Date)   (Office)

(20) Signature of person preparing form, if other than applicant. I declare that this document was prepared by me at the request of the applicant and is based on all information of which I have any knowledge.

SIGNATURE:

ADDRESS:	DATE:

(SIGN HERE) *Maria Ulloa - Contreras*
(Signature of applicant or parent or guardian)

(3)

folleto, **Formulario N-17,** "Los Requisitos de Naturalización e Informe General", y en particular, la sección de "Naturalización para Niños". Para obtener uno de éstos folletos gratis, refiérase a la siguiente sección aqui abajo, **Dónde Obtener Una Solicitud.**

El Formulario N-600 es para las personas que ya son cuidadanas a través de otra persona, tal como el marido o el padre, pero que desean un certificado para enseñar una prueba de ciudadanía. Las circunstancias son muy variables en casos de ciudadanía por "adquisición", pero si usted piensa que ya es ciudadano de los Estados Unidos a través de su cónyuge o padre, entonces llene el Formulario N-600 para solicitar su Certificado de Ciudadanía. Si no está muy seguro, entonces sería mejor buscar primero a un consejero experto de cualquier oficiana del INS o a un abogado de Inmigración antes de entregar su solicitud.

El ejemplar 4 le muestra la Forma N-600. Puede ser presentada por un solicitante adulto, o se puede presentar por un padre o tutor a nombre de un niño. No se le exige que se inicie esta solicitud del todo. Es enteramente voluntario, y si no entrega un N-600 no afecta en ninguna forma la ciudadanía de una persona. Un honorario de $60.00 se tiene que entregar junto con la solicitud, y no se le devolverá no importa que acción se tome sobre la solicitud. Además del honora rio, usted debe de entregar junto con su solicitud, tres fotos y cualquier prueba de nacimiento, muerte, divorcio, adopción y otras cosas esenciales en forma de certificado o documentos para comprobar su reclamo a la ciudadanía a través del matrimonio o de los padres.

En resumen, la mayoría de las personas, al cumplir con los 8 requisitos de naturalización, usarán el Fomulario N-400, "Solicitud para Iniciar la Petición de Naturalización". Si piensa usted necesitar alguna otra solicitud para un caso especial, póngase en contacto con su oficiana del INS que le quede más cerca y pregúnteles. En esta forma usted puede estar absolutamente seguro de conseguir la solicitud correcta desde el principio.

Dónde conseguir una solicitud

Se puede obtener una solicitud en persona o por correo de su

section "Naturalization of Children." To obtain one of these free pamphlets, refer to the next section, **Where to get an application**.

Form N-600 is for people who are already citizens through someone else, like a husband or parent, but desire a certificate to show proof of their citizenship. The circumstances vary greatly in cases of citizenship through "acquisition," but if you think that you are already a citizen of the United States through a spouse or parent, then fill out Form N-600 to apply for your Certificate of Citizenship. If you are not certain, it would be best to first seek expert advice from any INS office or from an immigration attorney before submitting this application.

Sample 4 shows Form N-600. It can be filed by an adult applicant, or it can be filed by a parent or guardian on behalf of a child. It is not required that you file this application at all. It is entirely voluntary; failure to submit an N-600 does not in any way affect a person's citizenship. A fee of $60.00 must be submitted along with the application, and it will not be refunded regardless of the action taken on the application. In addition to this fee, you must also submit evidence of birth, marriage, death, divorce, adoption, and other essential matters in the form of certificates or documents to prove your claim to citizenship through marriage or parents.

In summary, the majority of people, having met the eight general requirements for naturalization, will use Form N-400, "Application to File Petition for Naturalization." If you think you may need some other application for your special case, contact your nearest INS office and ask. This way, you will be absolutely certain to acquire the correct application right from the start.

Where to get an application

An application can be obtained in person or by mail from your nearest Immigration and Naturalization Service office. See Appendix 4, "INS Offices in the U.S.A." and Appendix 5, "INS Offices Overseas" for a complete listing including telephone numbers. Sometimes Pass-

oficina del Servicio de Inmigración y Naturalización más cercana. Véase Apéndice 4, "Oficinas del INS en los E.U.A." y el Apéndice 5, "Oficinas del INS de Ultramar" para ver una lista completa que incluye los números de teléfono. A veces, las oficinas de Pasaportes que se encuentran en la oficina del Secretario o Dependiente del Condado contienen una provisión de solicitudes, pero debe de llamar primero para mayor seguridad. Una ventaja que tiene el ir en persona es que puede recoger una cópia de ese folleto útil de referencias, el Formulario N-17, "Los Requisitos de Naturalización e Información General", mientras que se encuentra usted allí. Otra ventaja es que también le pueden hacer su Carta de Huellas digitales, lo cual le ahorra tiempo más adelante. Sin embargo, si le es más fácil escribir pidiendo estas cosas, sólo puede copiar la carta que se le muestra en el ejemplar 5, pero asegúrese de usar la dirección de la oficina del INS que le queda más cerca.

Cuándo debe uno pedir la solicitud

Algunos inmigrantes pueden desear hacerse ciudadanos tan pronto como sea posible. Otros pueden vivir en los Estados Unidos por años, y quizá, la mayoría de sus vidas antes de decidirse hacerse ciudadanos. Mientras que nunca es demasiado tarde comenzar el procedimiento de la solicitud, sí es posible comenzarlo demasiado temprano. Tiene usted primero que llenar el requisito de residencia por 5 años, o 3 años si está casado con ciudadano, antes de solicitar la naturalización.

Para mayor eficiencia, puede usted conseguir una solicitud unos cuantos meses antes de cumplir el requisito de la residencia. Usted puede enviar por correo o entregar personalmente su solicitud llena hasta 3 meses antes de la fecha en gue usted haya cumplido con el requisito de residencia. Ya que la losicitud es larga y toma bastante tiempo para llenarla, es buen plan para los que desean solicitar la ciudadanía lo más pronto posible. Tenga en mente que una vez que se entregue su solicitud, puede tardar mucho tiempo, probablemente más de un año, para que se tramite. Así es que mientras más pueda recibir su solicitud la oficina del Servicio de Inmigración y Naturalización que le queda más cerca, tendrá usted la preferencia de estar entre los más altos en la lista y así puede tramitarse más pronto.

port Offices located in your local County Clerk's office keep a supply of applications, but call first to make sure. An advantage to going personally is that you can pick up a copy of that handy reference pamphlet, Form N-17, "Naturalization Requirements and General Information," while you are there. Another advantage is that you can also get your fingerprint chart done, which saves time later on. However, if it is easier to write for these things, just copy the letter as shown in Sample 5, but be careful to use the address of the INS office closest to you.

When to apply

Some immigrants may wish to become citizens at the earliest possible time. Others may live in the United States for years, maybe even most of their lives, before deciding to become citizens. While it is never too late to begin the application process, it is possible to begin too early. You must first meet the residency requirement of 5 years, or 3 years if married to a citizen, before applying for naturalization.

For extra efficiency, you can get an application and begin filling it out a few months prior to meeting your residency requirement. You may mail or personally deliver your completed application up to 3 months before the date you actually meet your residency requirement. Because the application is lengthy and takes considerable time to fill out, this is a good plan for those desiring to apply for citizenship at the earliest possible time. Bear in mind that once your application has been submitted, it can take a long time to be processed. So the sooner the Immigration and Naturalization Service office receives your application, the higher up on the waiting list your application will be, and the sooner it can be processed.

How to complete the application

Instructions come with Form N-400, your "Application to File Petition for Naturalization." See Sample 6, "Instructions to the Applicant." Follow these instructions carefully and exactly. Use a typewriter if possible, or print neatly in ink. All items on the form should

Cómo completar la solicitud

Las instrucciones se incluyen con el Formulario N-400, su "Solicitud para Iniciar la Petición de Naturalización". Véase el ejemplar 6, "Instrucciones para el Solicitante". Siga usted estas instrucciones cuidadosamente y exactamente. Use una máquina de escribir si es posible, o escríbalo en tinta con letra de molde. Todos los artículos de la forma se deben de contestar a su mejor capacidad. Si alguna pregunta no le es pertinente, no deje un espacio en blanco. Escriba, "not applicable", que quiere decir, no me es pertinente.

Puede ser que le ayude el que mire usted el ejemplar 1 cuando esté llenando su propia solicitud. Si alguna persona lo ayuda a llenarla, esté seguro que usted haya comprendido completamente cada pregunta y que la haya contestado con cuidado, totalmente y correctamente. Las preguntas y respuestas de su solicitud serán una parte importante de su examen de naturalización por el cual determinará su escudriñador su dominio del inglés hablado.

Tres cosas merecen tener su atención especial cuando esté llenando su solicitud. Según al menos uno de los oficiales de la inmigración, son cosas de las que los solicitantes se descuidan comunmente y las hacen incorrectamente.

1. **Consistencia:** Esté seguro de escribir su nombre exactamente igual en todas partes de la solicitud entera con excepción de la línea donde le preguntan qué otros nombres ha usado.
2. **Arrestos:** Si le son pertinentes, llene el artículo 28 en la página tres totalmente y correctamente, aunque sea por una violación del tránsito. No lo deje en blanco si alguna vez ha sido arrestado. Esto es súmamente importante, ya que una omisión aquí puede poner en peligro su naturalización. Séa usted totalmente honrado!
3. **Organizaciones:** El artículo 29 en la página tres es importante. Si pertenece a clubs y a grupos ésto puede atestiguar que está usted capacitado para la ciudadanía. Es importante que mencione cualquier grupo.

be answered to the best of your ability. If a question is not applicable, do not leave it blank. Write "not applicable."

It may be helpful for you to refer to Sample 1 while filling out your own application. If someone helps you fill it out, make sure that you completely understand every question and have answered carefully, accurately and completely. The questions and answers on your application will be an important part of your naturalization examination whereby the examiner determines your mastery of spoken English.

Three items deserve your special attention when filling out your application. They are, according to at least one immigration official, items most commonly neglected or done incorrectly by applicants:

1. **Consistency:** Make sure your name is put down exactly the same throughout the entire application, except for the line that asks for other names you have used.
2. **Arrests:** If applicable, fill in item 28 on page 3 completely and accurately, even for a traffic violation. Do not leave it empty if you have ever been arrested. This is extremely important, as an omission here could jeopardize your naturalization. Be completely honest!
3. **Organizations:** Item 29 on page 3 is important. Your membership in clubs and groups can help attest to your suitability for citizenship. Do not consider it unimportant and overlook any group.

Aside from the application itself, you will need to complete the fingerprint chart and get photographs to specifications as follows:

The fingerprint chart

Before you write anything at all on the card, notice that the instructions on your application say that your signature must be given in the presence of the officer fingerprinting you. Do not sign the card until told to do so by the fingerprinting officer.

Sample 5
Sample Letter to Ob tain an Application

(Your street address)
(Your city, state, zip)

(Today's date)

Immigration & Naturalization Service
(Street address)
(City, state, zip code)

Dear Sir:

I want to become a United States citizen.

Please mail to the above address Form N-17, "Naturalization Requirements and General Information" and also Form N-400, "Application to File Petition for Naturalization" with the fingerprint chart and "Biographic Information" form.

I look forward to receiving these things at your earliest convenience. Thank you.

Sincerely,

(Your signature)
(Your name)

Example of a Fingerprint Card

APPLICANT	LEAVE BLANK	TYPE OR PRINT ALL INFORMATION IN BLACK

APPLICANT

LEAVE BLANK

TYPE OR PRINT ALL INFORMATION IN BLACK
LAST NAME NAM   FIRST NAME   MIDDLE NAME

FBI   LEAVE BLANK

SIGNATURE OF PERSON FINGERPRINTED

ALIASES AKA

ORI
CAINSSF00
USINS
SAN FRAN, CA

DATE OF BIRTH DOB
Month   Day   Year

RESIDENCE OF PERSON FINGERPRINTED

CITIZENSHIP CTZ

SEX | RACE | HGT. | WGT. | EYES | HAIR | PLACE OF BIRTH POB

DATE   SIGNATURE OF OFFICIAL TAKING FINGERPRINTS

YOUR NO. OCA

LEAVE BLANK

EMPLOYER AND ADDRESS

FBI NO. FBI

CLASS

ARMED FORCES NO. MNU

REASON FINGERPRINTED

SOCIAL SECURITY NO. SOC

REF.

MISCELLANEOUS NO. MNU

1. R. THUMB	2. R. INDEX	3. R. MIDDLE	4. R. RING	5. R. LITTLE
6. L. THUMB	7. L. INDEX	8. L. MIDDLE	9. L. RING	10. L. LITTLE

LEFT FOUR FINGERS TAKEN SIMULTANEOUSLY   L. THUMB | R. THUMB   RIGHT FOUR FINGERS TAKEN SIMULTANEOUSLY

Sample 6 – Form N-400
Instructions to the Applicant

U.S. Department of Justice
Immigration and Naturalization Service

OMB #1115-0009
Application for Naturalization

INSTRUCTIONS

Purpose of This Form.
This form is for use to apply to become a naturalized citizen of the United States.

Who May File.
You may apply for naturalization if:
- you have been a lawful permanent resident for five years;
- you have been a lawful permanent resident for three years, have been married to a United States citizen for those three years, and continue to be married to that U.S. citizen;
- you are the lawful permanent resident child of United States citizen parents; or
- you have qualifying military service.

Children under 18 may automatically become citizens when their parents naturalize. You may inquire at your local Service office for further information. If you do not meet the qualifications listed above but believe that you are eligible for naturalization, you may inquire at your local Service office for additional information.

General Instructions.
Please answer all questions by typing or clearly printing in black ink. Indicate that an item is not applicable with "N/A". If an answer is "none," write "none". If you need extra space to answer any item, attach a sheet of paper with your name and your alien registration number (A#), if any, and indicate the number of the item.

Every application must be properly signed and filed with the correct fee. If you are under 18 years of age, your parent or guardian must sign the application.

If you wish to be called for your examination at the same time as another person who is also applying for naturalization, make your request on a separate cover sheet. Be sure to give the name and alien registration number of that person.

Initial Evidence Requirements.
You must file your application with the following evidence:

A copy of your alien registration card.

Photographs. You must submit two color photographs of yourself taken within 30 days of this application. These photos must be glossy, unretouched and unmounted, and have a white background. Dimension of the face should be about 1 inch from chin to top of hair. Face should be 3/4 frontal view of right side with right ear visible. Using pencil or felt pen, lightly print name and A#, if any, on the back of each photo. This requirement may be waived by the Service if you can establish that you are confined because of age or physical infirmity.

Fingerprints. If you are between the ages of 14 and 75, you must sumit your fingerprints on Form FD-258. Fill out the form and write your Alien Registration Number in the space marked "Your No. OCA" or "Miscellaneous No. MNU". Take the chart and these instructions to a police station, sheriff's office or an office of this Service, or other reputable person or organization for fingerprinting. (You should contact the police or sheriff's office before going there since some of these offices do not take fingerprints for other government agencies.) You must sign the chart in the presence of the person taking your fingerprints and have that person sign his her name, title, and the date in the space provided. Do not bend, fold, or crease the fingerprint chart.

U.S. Military Service. If you have ever served in the Armed Forces of the United States at any time, you must submit a completed Form G-325B. If your application is based on your military service you must also submit Form N-426, "Request for Certification of Military or Naval Service."

Application for Child. If this application is for a permanent resident child of U.S. citizen parents, you must also submit copies of the child's birth certificate, the parents' marriage certificate, and evidence of the parents' U.S. citizenship. If the parents are divorced, you must also submit the divorce decree and evidence that the citizen parent has legal custody of the child.

Where to File.
File this application at the local Service office having jurisdiction over your place of residence.

Fee.
The fee for this application is $90.00. The fee must be submitted in the exact amount. It cannot be refunded. DO NOT MAIL CASH.

All checks and money orders must be drawn on a bank or other institution located in the United States and must be payable in United States currency. The check or money order should be made payable to the Immigration and Naturalization Service, except that:
- If you live in Guam, and are filing this application in Guam, make your check or money order payable to the "Treasurer, Guam."
- If you live in the Virgin Islands, and are filing this application in the Virgin Islands, make your check or money order payable to the "Commissioner of Finance of the Virgin Islands."

Checks are accepted subject to collection. An uncollected check will render the application and any document issued invalid. A charge of $5.00 will be imposed if a check in payment of a fee is not honored by the bank on which it is drawn.

Form N-400 (Rev. 07/17/91) N

Processing Information.
Rejection. Any application that is not signed or is not accompanied by the proper fee will be rejected with a notice that the application is deficient. You may correct the deficiency and resubmit the application. However, an application is not considered properly filed until it is accepted by the Service.

Requests for more information. We may request more information or evidence. We may also request that you submit the originals of any copy. We will return these originals when they are no longer required.

Interview. After you file your application, you will be notified to appear at a Service office to be examined under oath or affirmation. This interview may not be waived. If you are an adult, you must show that you have a knowledge and understanding of the history, principles, and form of government of the United States. There is no exemption from this requirement.

You will also be examined on your ability to read, write, and speak English. If on the date of your examination you are more than 50 years of age and have been a lawful permanent resident for 20 years or more, or you are 55 years of age and have been a lawful permanent resident for at least 15 years, you will be exempt from the English language requirements of the law. If you are exempt, you may take the examination in any language you wish.

Oath of Allegiance. If your application is approved, you will be required to take the following oath of allegiance to the United States in order to become a citizen:

"I hereby declare, on oath, that I absolutely and entirely renounce and abjure all allegiance and fidelity to any foreign prince, potentate, state or sovereignty, of whom or which I have heretofore been a subject or citizen; that I will support and defend the Constitution and laws of the United States of America against all enemies, foreign and domestic; that I will bear true faith and allegiance to the same; that I will bear arms on behalf of the United States when required by the law; that I will perform noncombatant service in the armed forces of the United States when required by the law; that I will perform work of national importance under civilian direction when required by the law; and that I take this obligation freely without any mental reservation or purpose of evasion; so help me God."

If you cannot promise to bear arms or perform noncombatant service because of religious training and belief, you may omit those statements when taking the oath. "Religious training and belief" means a person's belief in relation to a Supreme Being involving duties superior to those arising from any human relation, but does not include essentially political, sociological, or philosophical views or merely a personal moral code.

Oath ceremony. You may choose to have the oath of allegiance administered in a ceremony conducted by the Service or request to be scheduled for an oath ceremony in a court that has jurisdiction over the applicant's place of residence. At the time of your examination you will be asked to elect either form of ceremony. You will become a citizen on the date of the oath ceremony and the Attorney General will issue a Certificate of Naturalization as evidence of United States citizenship.

If you wish to change your name as part of the naturalization process, you will have to take the oath in court.

Penalties.
If you knowingly and willfully falsify or conceal a material fact or submit a false document with this request, we will deny the benefit you are filing for, and may deny any other immigration benefit. In addition, you will face severe penalties provided by law, and may be subject to criminal prosecution.

Privacy Act Notice.
We ask for the information on this form, and associated evidence, to determine if you have established eligibility for the immigration benefit you are filing for. Our legal right to ask for this information is in 8 USC 1439, 1440, 1443, 1445, 1446, and 1452. We may provide this information to other government agencies. Failure to provide this information, and any requested evidence, may delay a final decision or result in denial of your request.

Paperwork Reduction Act Notice.
We try to create forms and instructions that are accurate, can be easily understood, and which impose the least possible burden on you to provide us with information. Often this is difficult because some immigration laws are very complex. Accordingly, the reporting burden for this collection of information is computed as follows: (1) learning about the law and form, 20 minutes; (2) completing the form, 25 minutes; and (3) assembling and filing the application (includes statutory required interview and travel time, after filing of application), 3 hours and 35 minutes, for an estimated average of 4 hours and 20 minutes per response. If you have comments regarding the accuracy of this estimate, or suggestions for making this form simpler, you can write to both the Immigration and Naturalization Service, 425 I Street, N.W., Room 5304, Washington, D.C 20536; and the Office of Management and Budget, Paperwork Reduction Project, OMB No. 1115-0009, Washington, D.C. 20503.

Aparte de la solicitud misma, necesitará completar la Carta de huellas digitales y tendrá que obtener fotos recientes conforme a las especificaciones que siguen:

La Carta De Huellas Digitales

Antes de que escriba usted cualquier cosa sobre esta tarjeta, dése cuenta que las instrucciones sobre su solicitud dicen que su firma se tendrá que dar en la presencia del oficial que le tome sus huellas digitales. No firme la tarjeta al menos que el oficial tomando sus huellas digitales se lo indique.

Si recoge su solicitud en persona, el Formulario N-400, de una oficina del Servicio de Inmigración y Naturalización le pueden tomar allí mismo e inmediatamente sus huellas digitales. Esta es la manera de hacerlo con más eficiencia. Es gratis y usted se ahorrará un viaje especial más tarde para sólo tomar las huellas digitales. Pero si usted manda su solicitud por correo y la oficina del INS que le queda más cerca está bastante lejos, llame a la oficina de su sheriff o a la estación de la policía. La policía del Estado generalmente hace mejores Cartas de huellas digitales que la policía local. Cuando llame, pídales si le pueden tomar sus huellas digitales para su solicitud de ciudadanía y que si le cobrarán, y a que hora y en que día le pueden tomar sus huellas digitales.

Debe usted de llenar toda la información de antecedentes personales de la tarjeta de las huellas digitales tal como se le explica en el artículo 2 de las "Instrucciones al Solicitante". Entonces cargue con su tarjeta y su hoja de instrucciones cuando vaya a que le tomen sus huellas digitales. Sólo se puede usar la tarjeta que le provee el INS. Firme su nombre en frente del oficial. Y esté seguro de no doblar, plegar o arrugar la Carta de huellas digitales.

Las buenas huellas digitales son importantes! Si no se las toman bien le puede retardar su solicitud. Asi es que verifique para estar seguro que la Carta de huellas digitales tiene:
- Las primeras dos conyunturas del dedo que aparece sobre la tarjeta, no sólo la punta del dedo.

If you pick up your application, Form N-400, personally at an Immigration and Naturalization Service office, you can get your fingerprints done then and there. This is the most efficient way. It is free and will save you a special trip just for fingerprints later on. But if you sent for your application by mail, and your nearest INS office is quite far away, call your local sheriff's office or police station. State police generally provide better fingerprints than local police. When you call, ask them if they can take your fingerprints for your citizenship application, if there is any cost, and what time and on what days they do fingerprints.

You should fill out all the personal data information of the fingerprint chart as stated in item 2 of "Instructions to the Applicant." Then take both your card and your instruction sheet with you when you go to have your fingerprints taken. Only the card supplied by the INS may be used. Sign your name in front of the "officer." And be sure not to bend, fold, or crease the fingerprint chart.

Good fingerprints are important! A poor set could delay your application. So check to make sure that your fingerprint chart has:
- The first two joints of the finger appearing on the card, not just the finger tip.
- The proper amount of ink, as too much ink causes smears. Too little ink cannot be deciphered.
- Neat and clear prints, as sloppy looking prints are probably bad prints and will generally be rejected.

In addition to getting a good set of fingerprints on your chart, you will also need the required photographs.

Photographs

First of all, plan to have your pictures taken within the last 30 days prior to submitting your application. When you are ready, you will find that photographers are usually very familiar with the specifications for the 3 photos. However, just to be on the safe side when you go to the photographer, take with you your "Instructions to the Appli-

- Una cantidad adecuada de tinta ya que usando demasiada tinta causa manchas y usando poca no se alcanza a ver.
- Impresiones limpias y claras, ya que las impresiones mal hechas probablemente no se considerarán y en general, las rechazarán.

Además de conseguir un buen grupo de huellas digitales sobre su Carta, tambien necesitará las fotos exigidas.

Fotografías

Primeramente, haga plan para que le tomen sus retratos dentro de los ultimos 30 días antes de entregar su solicitud. Cuando esté listo, se dará cuenta que los fotógrafos normalmente conocen bien las especificaciones de las 3 fotos. Sin embargo, para estar más seguro, cuando vaya con un fotógrafo, cargue con su hoja de "Instrucciones al Solicitante" para referirse al artículo 1, "Fotografías de su Cara". Algunos fotógrafos aceptan a cualquier momento que una persona llegue y le tienen sus fotos en minutos. Debe de llamar usted primero para ver si necesita una cita. Al recibir las 3 fotos, escriba suavemente con lápiz inmediatamente su número de la "Mica" junto con su nombre en la parte de atrás y en el centro de cada una. Recuerde que una vez que haya tomado sus fotos, tiene usted un máximo de 30 días para mandarlas por correo o para entregarlas en persona junto con su solicitud entera que haya completado a la oficina del Servicio de Inmigración y Naturalización.

La entrega de la solicitud

Antes de entregar su solicitud completa, sea en persona o por correo, primero arranque la hoja de "Instrucciones al Solicitante". Luego junte todas las partes de su solicitud. Suponiendo que usó usted el N-400, entonces debe de tener:

1. La Solicitud para Iniciar la Petición de Naturalización, Formulario N-400.
2. La Hoja de Información Biográfica, G-325.
3. La Carta de Huellas Digitales.
4. Las tres fotografías.
5. Un cheque o giro por $60.00 pagaderos al "Immigration and

cant" sheet for reference to item 1, "Photographs of your Face." Some photographers take walk-ins and have your pictures ready in minutes. You should call first to ask if you need an appointment. Upon receiving the 3 photos, immediately write your Alien Registration number lightly in pencil on the back center of each one. Remember, once you have your photos, you have no more than 30 days in which to mail or personally deliver your entire, completed application to the Immigration and Naturalization Service office.

Submitting the completed application

Before you submit your completed application, whether in person or by mail, first tear off the "Instructions to the Applicant" sheet. Next, assemble all the parts of your application together. Assuming you used N-400, you should have:

1. The Application to File Petition for Naturalization, Form N-400.
2. The Biographic Information Sheet, G-325.
3. The Fingerprint Chart.
4. The 3 Photographs.
5. A check or money order for $90.00 payable to the "Immigration and Naturalization Service. (It is a good idea to write your Alien Registration number on your check or money order.)
6. Any required accompanying documents.

For any "accompanying documents," the INS no longer requires that you submit only *original* or *certified copies* of documents you send with the application. Now you may send legible photocopies, but you must attach your signed statement worded as follows:

Copies of documents submitted are exact photocopies of unaltered original documents, and I understand that I may be required to submit original documents to an Immigration or Consular official at a later date.

_____   _____
              Signature   Date

Naturalization Service." (Es buena idea escribir su número de Registro como Extranjero en su cheque o giro.)

6. Cualquier documentación que debe de acompañarlos. No mande dinero con su solicitud.

Para cualesquier "documentos que la acompañen," el INS no requiere ya que usted entregue solamente originales o copias certificadas de los documentos que mande usted con la solicitud. Ahora puede usted mandar copias fotostáticas legibles, pero debe usted añadir la siguiente declaración firmada con la siguiente redacción:

Las copias de los documentos entregados son copias fotostáticas de documentos originales no adulterados, y yo entiendo que se me puede pedir que presente los documentos originales a un funcionario de Inmigración o Consular en una fecha posterior.

_____   _____
Firma   Fecha

Antes de que salga de sus manos su solicitud, haga fotocopias de todo. En ésta forma tendrá usted el duplicado para usarlo como referencia al preparar su examen preliminar, el cual es el segundo paso del procedimiento de naturalización. Tambien, al guardar usted su copia, tendrá algo de referencia si a caso se le pierde la solicitud que entregó.

Si manda por correo su solicitud, use un sobre grande, preferiblemente uno que mida 9 por 12 pulgadas. Escriba la dirección de la oficina del INS que le queda más cerca y ponga su propia dirección en la esquina alta del lado izquierdo del sobre. Haga que el dependiente postal le pese su sobre para determinar la cantidad exacta que necesita de porte. Debido a la importancia del contenido, puede decidir usted mandarlo por "correo certificado con acuse de recibo". En éste forma tiene usted una verificación que el INS recibió su solicitud. Una vez que su solicitud esté fuera de sus manos, entonces le viene una espera muy, muy larga.

Puede usted utilizar bien su tiempo de espera. Uselo para aprender algunos hechos básicos de la historia de los Estados Unidos y de su gobierno. Este conocimiento lo necesita ud. para poder pasar el examen preliminar, que es el siguiente paso grande camino a la ciudadanía de los Estados Unidos.

Before your application leaves your hands, make a photocopy of everything. This way you will have it for reference in preparation for your preliminary examination, which is step two in the process of naturalization. Also, by keeping a copy for yourself you will have something to refer to in case the application you submitted is lost.

If you mail your application (rather than personally delivering it), use a large envelope, preferably a size 9 x 12 inches. Address it to your nearest INS office and put your return address in the upper left corner of the envelope. Have the postal clerk weigh your envelope to determine the exact amount of postage. Because of the importance of the contents, you may decide to send it by "certified" mail with a return receipt. This way, you have verification that the INS did receive your application. Once the application is out of your hands, there comes a wait, sometimes a long one.

Your waiting time can be put to good use. Use it to learn the basic facts about United States history and government. This knowledge is required in order for you to pass the preliminary examination, the next big step on the way to becoming a United States citizen.

Capitulo 3
EL EXAMEN PRELIMINAR

Despues de entregar su solicitud terminada, sea por correo o en persona al Servicio de Inmigración y Naturalización, puede usted contar con una espera larga de al menos varios meses antes de que le notifiquen cuándo y adonde debe de comparecer para su examen preliminar. Cada persona que solicita su naturalización sin excepción, tiene que tomar este examen, el cual forma el segundo paso, camino a su ciudadanía.

La naturaleza del examen

Un escudriñador de naturalización le hará preguntas sobre su solicitud, el Formulario N-400 para estar seguro de que esté completo y en el debida orden para registrarlo con la corte. Le harán preguntas bajo juramento y el escrudiñador estará seguro que usted:

1. Reúna los requisitos de residencia y de presencia física,
2. de que sea usted una persona honrada,
3. de que no tenga alguna conexión con ninguna organización subversiva,
4. de que tenga conocimiento de la historia y el gobierno de los Estados, y
5. de que pueda leer, escribir y hablar el inglés.

El escudriñador de naturalización le hace las preguntas verbalmente en un inglés sencillo. Una razón principal para el capítulo 3 de éste libro es el ayudarle a aprender suficientemente de la historia y el gobierno de los Estados Unidos para que pueda tomar y terminar este examen. Hay 102 preguntas y contestaciones aquí abajo que cubren el conocimiento necesario.

Si le parece que usted reúne los requisitos para naturalizarse, entonces el escudriñador le pedirá que firme su solicitud, el Formulario N-400 en la sección que dice, "No llene ningun blanco debajo de ésta línea".

Chapter 3
THE PRELIMINARY EXAMINATION

After submitting your completed application by mail or in person to the Immigration and Naturalization Service, expect a wait of at least several months before being notified when and where to appear for the preliminary examination. Every person applying for naturalization, with no exceptions, must take this examination, which is step two on the way to citizenship.

The nature of the examination

A naturalization examiner will question you about your application, Form N-400, to make sure that it is complete and in proper order for filing with the court. You will be questioned under oath by an examiner in order to make certain that you:

1. meet the residency and physical presence requirements,
2. are of good moral character,
3. have no connection with any subversive organization,
4. have a knowledge of United States history and government, and
5. are able to read, write and speak English.

The questions are given orally, in simple English, by the naturalization examiner. One main goal of Chapter 3 of this book is to help you to learn enough about United States history and government so you can get through this examination. There are 102 questions and answers below which cover the necessary knowledge.

If it appears that you meet the requirements for naturalization, the examiner will ask you to sign your application, Form N-400, under the section, "Do Not Fill in Blanks Below This Line." It is then given to the clerk of the court who fills out a formal "Petition for Naturaliza-

Sample 7 – Form N-405
Petition for Naturalization

U.S. Department of Justice
Immigration and Naturalization Service

PETITION FOR NATURALIZATION

ORIGINAL (To be retained by Clerk of Court)

Petition No. __947785__

A.R. No. __A 55 416 038__

To the Honorable __Naturalization__ Court for the __U.S. District__ at __Los Angeles__

This petition for naturalization, hereby made and filed under section __316 (a)__
Immigration and Nationality Act, respectfully shows:

(1) My full, true, and correct name is __Pedro Garcia-Gonzalez__
(Full, true name, without abbreviations)

(2) My present place of residence is __621 E. Emmett St. Santa Ana__
(Apt. No.) *(Number and Street)* *(City or Town)*

__U.S.A.__ __California__ __92707__
(Country) *(State)* *(ZIP Code)*

(3) I was born on __Dec. 3, 1945__ in __San Pulco, Zacatecas, Mexico__

(4) I request that my name be changed to __Pete Garcia__

(5) I was lawfully admitted to the United States for permanent residence and have not abandoned such residence.

(6) [If petition filed under Section 316(a).] I have resided continuously in the United States for at least five years and continuously in the States in which this petition is made for at least six months, immediately preceding the date of this petition and after my lawful admission for permanent residence, and I have been physically present in the United States for at least one-half of such five year period.

(7) [If petition filed under Section 319(a).] I have resided continuously in the United States in marital union with my present spouse for at least three years immediately preceding the date of this petition, and after my lawful admission for permanent residence, during all of which period my said spouse has been a United States citizen, and have been physically present in the United States at least one-half of such three-year period. I have resided continuously in the States in which this petition is made at least six months immediately preceding the date of this petition.

(8) [If petition filed under Section 319(b).] My present spouse is a citizen of the United States, in the employment of the Government of the United States, or of an American institution of research recognized as such by the Attorney General, or an American firm or corporation engaged in whole or in part in the development of foreign trade and commerce of the United States, or subsidiary thereof, or of a public international organization in which the United States participates by treaty or statute, or is authorized to perform the ministerial or priestly functions of a religious denomination having a bona fide organization within the United States, or is engaged solely as a missionary by a religious denomination or by an interdenominational mission organization have a bona fide organization within the United States, and such spouse is regularly stationed abroad in such employment. I intend in good faith upon naturalization to live abroad with my spouse and to resume my residence within the United States immediately upon termination of such employment abroad.

(9) [If petition filed under Section 328.] I have served honorably in the Armed Forces of the United States for a period or periods aggregating three years. I have never been separated from the Armed Forces of the United States under other than honorable conditions. If not still in service, my service terminated within six months of the filing of my petition.

(10) [If petition filed under Section 329.] While an alien or noncitizen national of the United States, I served honorably in an active-duty status in the military, air, or naval forces of the United States during either World War I or during a period beginning September 1, 1939, and ending December 31, 1946, or during a period beginning June 25, 1950, and ending July 1, 1955, or during a period beginning February 28, 1961, and ending October 15, 1978, or I was discharged after five years of service under the Act of June 30, 1950 [P.L. 597, 81st Congress]. If separated from such service, I was separated under honorable conditions. At the time of enlistment, reenlistment, or induction I was in the United States, the Canal Zone, American Samoa, or Swains Island. If not in any of these places, I was lawfully admitted to the United States for permanent residence subsequent to enlistment or induction. I was never separated from such service on account of alienage. I was not a conscientious objector who performed no military, air, or naval duty whatever or refused to wear the uniform. I have not previously been naturalized on the basis of the same period of service.

(11) I am not and have not been, within the meaning of the Immigration and Nationality Act, for a period of at least 10 years immediately preceding the date of this petition, a member of or affiliated with any organization proscribed by such Act, or any section, subsidiary, branch, affiliate or subdivision thereof, nor have I during such period believed in, advocated, engaged in, or performed any of the acts or activities prohibited by such Act.

(12) I am, and have been during all the periods required by law, a person of good moral character, attached to the principles of the Constitution of the United States and well disposed to the good order and happiness of the United States.

(13) It is my intention in good faith to become a citizen of the United States and take without qualification the oath of renunciation and allegiance prescribed by the Immigration and Nationality Act, and to reside permanently in the United States. I am willing, when required by law, to bear arms on behalf of the United States, to perform noncombatant service in the Armed Forces of the United States, and to perform work of national importance under civilian director [unless exempted therefrom].

(14) I am able to read, write, and speak the English language [unless exempted therefrom], and I have a knowledge and understanding of the fundamentals of the history, and of the principles and form of government of the United States.

(15) Wherefore I request that I may be admitted a citizen of the United States of America. I swear [affirm] that I know the contents of this petition for naturalization subscribed by me, and that the same are true to the best of my knowledge and belief, and that this petition is signed by me with my full, true name. So help me God.

(16)

Pedro Garcia-Gonzalez
(Full Name, Without Abbreviations)

When Oath Administered by Clerk or Deputy Clerk of Court	When Oath Administered by Designated Examiner
Subscribed and sworn to (affirmed) before me by above-named petitioner in the respective forms of oath shown in said petition and affidavit, and filed by said petitioner, in the office of the clerk of said court at _____	Subscribed and sworn to (affirmed) before me by above-name petitioner in the respective forms of oath shown in said petition and affaidvit at _____ this _____ day of _____ , 19 ____
this _____ day of _____ , 19 ____	
_____ Clerk.	*Designated Examiner.*
_____ Deputy Clerk.	I HEREBY CERTIFY that the foregoing petition for naturalization was by petioner named herein filed in the office of the clerk of said court at _____ this _____ day of _____ , 19 ____
	_____ Clerk.
	_____ Deputy Clerk.

[SEAL] (SAMPLE)

Form N-405 (Rev. 06/03/87) Y

AMERICAN HOLIDAYS

New Year's Day

Lincoln's Birthday

Washington's Birthday

Memorial Day

Independence Day

Flag Day

Citizenship Day

Labor Day

Martin Luther King, Jr. Day

Veterans Day

Election Day

Thanksgiving

Christmas

Entonces se le entrega al secretario de la corte y él llena una planilla formal "La Petición para Naturalización", el Formulario N-405, tal como se ve en el ejemplar no. 7. Usted va a leer esta petición cuidadosamente, entonces la firmará y tomará juramento del mismo.

Se les pide a los hijos que automáticamente se vuelven ciudadanos a través de la naturalización de sus padres y que tengan los años necesarios para poder firmar un Certificado de Ciudadanía que estén presentes para el examen de sus padres. Sin embargo no se les exige pasar el examen de inglés o los requisitos de naturalización (se encuentran en el Capítulo 1).

Si usted no reune todos los requisitos para la naturalización, el escudriñador le dirá y, probablemente le recomendará que tome alguna acción para corregirlo. Por ejemplo, si su conocimiento del inglés o de la historia y el gobierno de los Estados Unidos no es bastante bueno, el escudriñador le puede sugerir que se le registre su petición de todas formas, pero que se le postergue su examen para una fecha en el futuro cuando esté usted mejor preparado. Si hay alguna deficiencia grave, el escudriñador le puede aconsejar que no registre usted la petición.

Ya no se necesitan testigos para el examen:

Un solicitante para naturalización ya no se le requiere que traiga testigos al examen.

Los requisitos escolares para pasar el examen:

Se le exige a un solicitante que tenga conocimiento del inglés, que pueda escribir y leerlo sencillamente y que tenga conocimiento de la historia y gobierno de los Estados Unidos. Hay ciertas excepciones a éstos requisitos, los cuales se explican en el Apéndice 6, "Informe Referente a la Escuela sobre la Ciudadanía para llenar los Requisitos de Naturalización".

La falta del conocimiento del inglés hablado, muy seguidamente es un obstáculo para llenar los requisitos educacionales de los ciudadanos anticipados. Verdaderamente, mucho del examen está diseñado para

tion," Form N-405, as shown in Sample 7. You will read this petition carefully, then sign the affidavit at the bottom and swear to it.

Children who automatically become citizens through their parents' naturalization and who are old enough to sign a Certificate of Citizenship are requested to attend their parents' examination. However, they are not required to pass the English test or the citizenship requirements of naturalization (listed in Chapter 1). Children under age 14 do not have to take the Oath of Allegiance.

If you do not meet all the requirements for naturalization, the examiner will tell you and probably recommend corrective action. For example, if your knowledge of English or United States history and government is not good enough, the examiner may suggest that your petition be filed anyway, but that the examination be postponed until a later date when you are better prepared. If there is a serious deficiency, the examiner may advise you not to file the petition.

Witnesses no longer required for the examination:

An applicant for naturalization is no longer required to bring witnesses to the examination.

Educational requirements to pass the examination:

An applicant is required to have a knowledge of English, simple writing and reading skills, and a knowledge of United States history and government. There are certain exceptions to the requirements, which are explained in Appendix 6, "Information Concerning Citizenship Education to Meet Naturalization Requirements."

Lack of knowledge of spoken English is often the biggest stumbling block in meeting the educational requirements for prospective citizens. In fact, much of the examination is designed to test your knowledge of simple English. An applicant may be asked only a few questions on history and government, and this generally takes just a small portion of the time at the preliminary hearing. You will also be

examinar el conocimiento del inglés sencillo. A un solicitante se le pueden hacer unas pocas preguntas sobre la historia y el gobierno, y ésto en general toma sólo una porción pequeña del tiempo para el examen preliminar. Se le pedirá tambien que lea y escriba unas pocas frases o expresiones en inglés. La mayoría de la entrevista probablemente tendrá que ver con las preguntas sobre su solicitud. Normalmente las preguntas que le hacen son pocas y sencillas. Si el escudriñador tiene alguna duda de su conocimiento y comprensión de la historia y el gobierno de los Estados Unidos, entonces puede prolongar las preguntas.

Su dominio del inglés hablado es de suma importancia! Los reglamentos dicen que "la capacidad del peticionario para hablar el inglés se determinará por las respuestas y las preguntas que se hacen normalmente durante el curso de la entrevista preliminar" o el examen. Asi es que para poder llenar el requisito educacional, esté completamente familiarizado con las preguntas y las respuestas en el Formulario N-400 y el Formulario N-325 tambien. Esta es la razón que le servirá de mucho la fotoscópia que tomó de su solicitud antes de entregarla, como un estudio.

Además del requisito del idoma inglés, debe de tener un conocimiento básico de la historia y el gobierno de los E.U. "Gobierno" quiere decir básicamente la Constitución. Puede usted aprenderlo en casa al familiarizarse con las 102 preguntas y respuestas aquí abajo. Pruebe diferentes tácticas cuando las estudie. Primero, solo lea un grupo pequeño, como quizás 3 o 5 preguntas y respuestas, una y dos veces; segundo, léa solo las preguntas, cubriendo las respuestas. Vea cuánto alcanza a recordar. ¿Se le olvidó una? Mire otra vez la respuesta. Repase el grupo por la tercera vez, pero ésta vez, escriba cualquier respuesta que no pudo contestar. Estudie solo esas respuestas. A la cuarta vez, le saldrán probablemente todas bien y estará listo para seguir adelante con el grupo de 3 o 5 preguntas y respuestas que siguen, repitiendo el proceso.

Acuérdese, probablemente tendrá muchos meses para estudiar, conenzando desde el tiempo que entregó usted su solicitud, el Formulario N-400 hasta el tiempo de su examen preliminar. Esto le permite suficiente tiempo para estudiar sobre la historia y el gobierno de los Estados Unidos y prepararse para tomar su examen preliminar. Lea toda la Constitución

asked to read or write a few sentences or expressions in English. Most of the interview will probably be concerned with questions on your application. Ordinarily, the questions asked are few and simple. If the examiner has some doubt about your knowledge and understanding of United States history and government, the questioning could be prolonged.

Your mastery of spoken English is of vital importance! The regulations state that "the ability of a petitioner to speak English shall be determined from answers to questions normally asked in the course of the preliminary interview," or examination. Therefore, in order to meet the educational requirement, be thoroughly familiar with the questions and your answers on Form N-400 and Form N-325, too. This is why the photocopy you made of your application before submitting it will come in very handy for study purposes.

In addition to the English language requirement, you must have a basic knowledge of U.S. history and government. "Government" means, for the most part, the Constitution. You can accomplish this right at home by familiarizing yourself with the 102 questions and answers that follow. Try various techniques when you study them. First, just read through a small group, like maybe 3 or 5 questions and answers, once or twice. Second, read just the questions, with the answers covered up. See how much you remember. Forget one? Look at the answer again. Go through the group a third time, but this time write down any answer you missed. Study only those answers. By the fourth try, you will probably get them all right and be ready to take on the next group of 3 or 5 questions, repeating the procedure.

Remember, you will likely have many months from the time you submit your application Form N-400 until the time of your preliminary examination. This allows ample time to study about United States history and government in preparation for the preliminary examination. Read through the Constitution of the United States of America at least once. It appears in Appendix 7. It is truly a fascinating document which will not only add to your knowledge and understanding but also add to your appreciation of United States government.

de los Estados Unidos al menos una vez. Aparece en el Apéndice 7. Es un documento verdaderamente fascinante que no sólo le incrementará su conocimiento y su comprensión pero tambien su aprecio por el gobierno de los Estados Unidos.

Cuando reciba la notificación de que se presente para su audiencia preliminar, la cual incluye el examen, póngase a repasar otra vez las 102 preguntas y respuestas. Una buena manera de hacerlo es de pedirle a otra persona que le haga las preguntas en cualquier orden, y entonces dé usted las respuestas. Haga que esta persona le anote cualquier pregunta que no pudo contestar. Concéntrese en éstas antes de ir a tomar su examen. Si usted estudia seriamente estas preguntas y contestaciones, no tendrá ninguna razón por la cual temer. Vuelva a leer la Constitución y revise cuidadosamente su N-400, y estará usted listo!

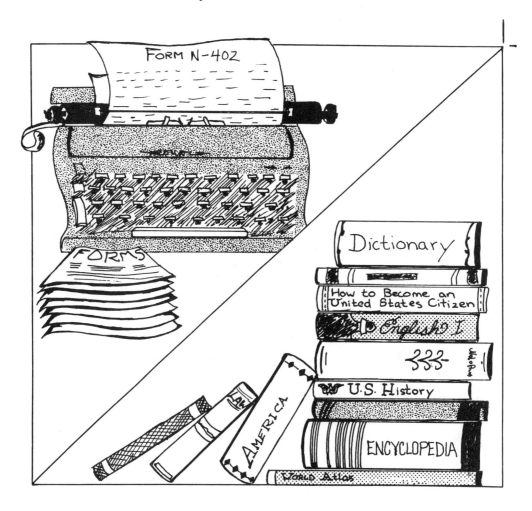

When you receive notification to appear for your preliminary hearing, which includes the examination, very carefully review the 102 questions and answers again. A good way to do this is to have another person ask you the questions, in any order, and **you** give the answers. Have that person keep a record of which questions you missed. Focus on those before going in for the examination. If you seriously study these questions and answers, you have no reason to be fearful. Re-read the Constitution and carefully look over your N-400, and you will be ready!

Growth of the Constitution

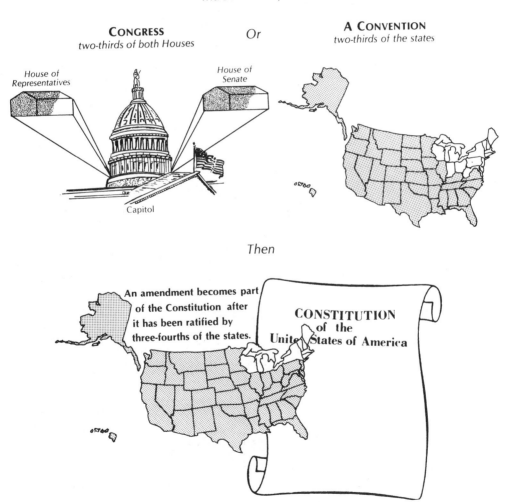

Introduced By . . .

CONGRESS
two-thirds of both Houses

Or

A CONVENTION
two-thirds of the states

House of Representatives

House of Senate

Capitol

Then

An amendment becomes part of the Constitution after it has been ratified by three-fourths of the states.

CONSTITUTION of the United States of America

102 preguntas y respuestas sobre la Historia de los E.U. y su Gobierno

Nota: En muchos casos, las respuestas que se dan parecen ser incompletas o incorrectas. Sin embargo, no importa lo que piense usted de ellas, éstas son las respuestas que espera oír el INS.

América, El Mundo Nuevo

1. ¿Cuándo se descubrió la América y por quién?

    En 1492, un Italiano llamado Cristobal Colón pensó incorrectamente que había llegado a la India pero en realidad, descubrio el "Nuevo Mundo", América.

2. ¿Por qué han venido a vivir a los Estados Unidos las gentes de todas partes del mundo?

    Han venido por muchas razones, pero principalmente para compartir totalmente las libertades que les ofrece los E.U. a sus ciudadanos.

3. ¿Dónde se fundó el primer poblado inglés en América?

    Se fundó en Jamestown, Virginia en el año 1607.

4. ¿Cuántas colonias primero formaron los E.U.?¿ Cuántas puede usted nombrar?

    En 1776, habían 13 colonias de la Gran Bretaña: Connecticut, Delaware, Georgia, Maryland, Massachusetts, New Hamshire, New Jersey, New York, North Carolina, Pennsylvania, Rhode Island, South Carolina y Virginia. Estas colonias se unieron y formaron los primeros E.U.

5. ¿Cuál fué la causa principal de la disputa entre las colonias y su patria, la Gran Bretaña?

    La Imposición de impuestos sin representación. Los colonos creían que era una gran injusticia forzarlos a pagar impuestos cuando nó tenían representación en el Parlamento Británico.

6. ¿Qué fue la Fiesta de Té de Boston?

    El Rey y el Parlamento al fin se pusieron de acuerdo para revocar todos los impuestos con excepción del que llevaba el té. Entonces,

102 Questions and Answers On U.S. History and Government

Note: In many cases, the answers given may seem incomplete or even inaccurate. However, whatever you may think of them, these are the answers expected by the INS.

America, The New World

1. When was America discovered and by whom?

   In 1492, an Italian by the name of Christopher Columbus mistakenly thought he had reached India but had in fact discovered the "New World," America.

2. Why have people from all over the world come to the United States to live?

   They have come for many reasons, but mainly to fully share in the freedoms the United States offers to its citizens.

3. Where was the first successful English settlement in America?

   It was founded in Jamestown, Virginia, in the year 1607.

4. How many colonies first made up the United States? How many can you name?

   In 1776, there were 13 British colonies: Connecticut, Delaware, Georgia, Maryland, Massachusetts, New Hampshire, New Jersey, New York, North Carolina, Pennsylvania, Rhode Island, South Carolina, and Virginia. These colonies joined together and became the first United States.

5. What was the main cause of dispute between the colonies and their "mother country," Great Britain?

   Taxation without representation. The colonists believed that it was especially unfair to force them to pay taxes when they had no representation in the British Parliament.

6. What was the Boston Tea Party?

   The King and Parliament finally agreed to repeal all of the taxes, except the one on tea. Then in 1773, The British East India

en 1773, la Compañía Británica de la India del Oriente mandó por barco millones de libras de té para los colonos. Los colonos nó permitían que se removiera el té de los barcos. Varios barcos regresaron a Gran Bretaña. En Boston, Massachussetts, los colonos subieron a los barcos y tiraron el té al mar en el puerto.

7. ¿Qué es la Declaración de Independencia?

Este documento famoso le anunció al mundo la separación y la independencia de las 13 colonias de la Gran Bretaña. Estas colonias primero se hicieron los 13 Estados y luego nacieron como los Estados Unidos de América.

8. ¿Quién escribió la Declaración de Independencia?

Tomás Jefferson, un miembro y líder del comité nombrado por el Segundo Congreso Continental para escribir la mayoría del escrito.

9. ¿Cuándo celebramos el cumpleaños de la nación?

El 4 de julio de 1776 marca el nacimiento de los Estados Unidos de América. El cuatro de Julio, conocido como el Día de la Independencia es una fiesta nacional y las gentes en los Estados Unidos celebran este día

10. ¿Cuándo y dónde se firmó la Declaración de Independencia?

El 4 de julio de 1776 fué aceptada por el Segundo Congreso Continental en Filadelfia pero no todos los delegados la firmaron hasta casi un mes después.

DECLARATION OF
INDEPENDENCE

LIBERTY
BELL

Company shipped millions of pounds of tea to the colonists. The colonists would not permit the tea to be removed from the ships. Several ships returned to Great Britain. In Boston, Massachusetts, the colonists boarded the ships and threw the tea in the harbor.

7. What is the Declaration of Independence?

    This famous document announced to the world the separation and independence of the 13 colonies from Great Britain. Those colonies became the first 13 states, and the United States of America was born.

8. Who wrote most of the Declaration of Independence?

    Thomas Jefferson, a leading member of a committee appointed by the Second Continental Congress, did most of the writing.

9. When do we celebrate our nation's birthday?

    July 4, 1776, marks the birth of the United States of America. The Fourth of July, known as Independence Day, is a national holiday, and people in the United States celebrate this day.

10. When and where was the Declaration of Independence signed?

    It was accepted by the Second Continental Congress in Philadelphia on July 4, 1776, but it was not signed by all delegates until almost a month later.

11. What was the Revolutionary War?

11. ¿Qué fué la Guerra Revolucionaria?

El Rey Jorge estaba enojado por la declaración de Independencia y decidió que la Gran Bretaña iba a pelear para retener las colonias. Mientras tanto, el Rey tenía dificultades en casa. La Gran Bretaña se encontraba en una guerra con España y Francia. En éste tiempo, Francia mandó ayuda a las colonias. La Guerra Revolucionaria fué una guerra larga y dura que terminó con la rendición del comandante Británico, Lord Cornwallis. Sin embargo, no fué hasta dos años despues, en 1783 que se firmó un trato de paz entre la Gran Bretaña y los nuevos Estados Unidos. Con este tratado Gran Bretaña reconoció a los Estados Unidos como nación independiente.

12. ¿Qué fueron los Artículos de la Confederación?

Los Artículos de la Confederación fue un documento y la primera prueba por las 13 colonias para establecer un gobierno propio. Ya que los Artículos no le dieron suficiente poder al gobierno central para poder parar las riñas entre los estados, se descartó y con ésto se abrió el camino para que se escribiera la Constitución de los Estados Unidos.

13. ¿Cuántos estados existen en los Estados Unidos y cuál es la capital?

Hay 50 estados, Washington, D.C. (Distrito de Colombia), que no es un estado, es la capital.

14. ¿Cuáles son los territorios de los Estados Unidos?

Puerto Rico, las Islas Vírgenes, Samoa y las Islas de Guam son territorios de los Estados Unidos. No se han ratificado como nuevos estados.

15. ¿Qué tan grandes son los Estados Unidos continentales?

Abarcan aproximadamente 2500 millas de la costa del Atlántico a la costa del Pacífico y aproximadamente 1300 millas del Canadá a México.

El Gobierno de los E.U.A.

16. ¿Qué forma de gobierno tienen los Estados Unidos?

El gobierno es una república, una república democrática, que la definió Abraham Lincoln como "un gobierno del pueblo, por el pueblo y para el pueblo".

King George was angered by the Declaration of Independence and decided that Great Britain would fight to keep the colonies. Meanwhile, the King had trouble at home, as Great Britain was at war with Spain and France. At this time France sent help to the colonies. The Revolutionary War was a long and hard war which ended with the surrender of the British commander, Lord Cornwalis. However, it was not until two years later, in 1783, that a peace treaty was signed between Great Britain and the new United States. By this treaty, Britain recognized the United States as an independent nation.

12. What were the Articles of Confederation?

The Articles of Confederation were the first attempt by the 13 colonies to set up self-government. Since the Articles did not give enough power to the central government to stop the quarreling among the states, they were discarded, and that paved the way for the writing of the Constitution of the United States.

13. How many states are there in the United States, and where is the capital?

There are 50 states. Washington, D.C. (District of Columbia), which is **not** a state, is the capital.

14. What are the territories of the United States?

Puerto Rico, the Virgin Islands, Samoa, and the Guam Islands are territories of the United States. They have not been ratified as new states.

15. How big is the continental United States?

It is approximately 2500 miles from the Atlantic coast to the Pacific coast and about 1300 miles from Canada to Mexico.

The Government of the U.S.A.

16. What is the form of government of the United States?

The government is a republic, or democratic republic, which was defined by Abraham Lincoln as "a government of the people, by the people, and for the people."

17. What are the 3 levels of government in the U.S.A.?

They are federal, state and local.

17. ¿Cuáles son los 3 niveles de gobierno en los E.U.A.?

    Son el federal, el estatal y el local.

18. ¿Qué es la Constitución?

    Es la "ley suprema de la tierra". La Constitución define la construcción y los poderes del gobierno federal. Las leyes estatales y locales no pueden estar en conflicto con la Constitución.

19. ¿Cuándo comenzó su vigencia la Constitución?

    Comenzó a funcionar bajo la Constitución en 1789.

20. ¿Puede cambiarse la Constitución?

    Sí, se pueden hacer cambios con adiciones que se llaman "enmiendas".

21. ¿Qué es el "Bill of Rights" (La Carta de Derechos)?

    Son las primeras 10 enmiendas de la Constitución. Todas las 10 se ratificaron (aprobaron) como un grupo en 1791.

22. ¿Cuáles son algunos de los más importantes derechos garantizados por el "Bill of Rights:?

    Entre otras cosas, el "Bill of Rights" protege la libertad de hablar, la libertad de la prensa, la libertad de la religión, el derecho de reunirse pacíficamente, y el derecho a un juicio justo.

23. ¿Cuántas enmiendas tiene la Constitución?

18. What is the Constitution?

It is the "supreme law of the land." The Constitution defines the construction and the powers of the federal government. State and local laws must not conflict with the Constitution.

19. When did the Constitution take effect?

The United States began to function under the Constitution in 1789.

20. Can the Constitution be changed?

Yes, changes can be made by additions called "amendments."

21. What is the Bill of Rights?

It is the first 10 amendments to the Constitution. All 10 were ratified (approved) as a group in 1791.

22. What are some very important rights guaranteed by the Bill of Rights?

Among other things, the Bill of Rights protects our freedom of speech, freedom of the press, freedom of religion, the right to peaceably assemble, and the right to a fair trial.

23. How many amendments has the Constitution?

There are 26 at present. Since the first 10, the Bill of Rights, there have been only 16 more amendments added since 1791.

Al tiempo presente tiene 26. Desde las primeras 10 que forman el "Bill of Rights", han habido sólo 16 enmiendas más añadidas desde 1791.

24. ¿Cuales son algunas de las más Importantes enmiendas del Bill of Rights?

No. 13 La revocación de la esclavitud

No. 19 Darles a las mujeres el derecho de votar

No. 22 Limitar al Presidente a dos períodos de 4 años en su puesto.

No. 26 Bajar la edad mínima para votar a 18 años.

25. ¿Cómo se puede enmendar la Constitución?

Las enmiendas pueden ser propuestas por dos terceras partes del voto de las Casas del Congreso o por una convención nacional llamada por el Congreso por petición de dos terceras partes del cuerpo legislativo estatal. Para volverse ley, las enmiendas entonces deben de ser ratificadas (aprobadas) por el cuerpo legislativo de tres cuartas partes de los estados.

26. ¿Cuantos años debe de tener un ciudadano para votar?

Un ciudadano debe de tener al menos 18 años según la Enmienda 26 (1971). Otro requisito adémas de la edad, es que cada votante debe de estar empadronado con la oficina de Registro de Votantes.

27. ¿Qué queremos decir con "el gobierno nacional"?

Queremos decir, el gobierno de un país en su totalidad en ves de los estados individuales.

28. ¿Se conoce el gobierno nacional por otro nombre?

Si, se llama el gobierno federal que quiere decir que los Estados Unidos son una unión o confederación de estados.

29. ¿Cuáles son algunos de los poderes del gobierno nacional?

* proveer para la defensa nacional
* hacer tratados y conducir relaciones con otros países
* reglamentar la inmigración y proveer la naturalización
* reglamentar el comercio con las naciones extranjeras y entre los estados
* acuñar moneda
* colectar impuestos federales, tales como el impuesto sobre los ingresos y el Seguro Social

24. What are some of the most important amendments after the Bill of Rights?

     No. 13 Abolished slavery

     No. 19 Gave women the right to vote

     No. 22 Limited the President to two 4-year terms in office

     No. 26 Lowered the minimum voting age to 18 years old

25. How can the Constitution be amended?

Amendments may be proposed by a two-thirds vote of both Houses of Congress or by a national convention called by Congress at the request of two-thirds of the state legislatures. To become law, amendments must then be ratified (approved) by the legislatures of three-fourths of the states or by special convention in three-fourths of the states.

26. How old must a citizen be to vote?

A citizen must be at least 18 years old according to Amendment 26 (1971). Another requirement, besides age, is that every voter be registered with the Registrar of Voters office.

27. What do we mean by "national" government?

We mean the government of the country as a whole, as opposed to individual states.

28. Is the national government called by any other name?

Yes, it is called the "federal" government which means the United States is a union, or federation, of states.

29. What are some of the powers of the national government?

* provide for the national defense
* make treaties and conduct relations with other countries
* regulate immigration and provide for naturalization
* regulate commerce with foreign nations and among the states
* coin money
* collect federal taxes, such as income tax and Social Security.

30. Into how many branches is the government of the United States divided, and what is the function of each?

    a. Legislative Branch (Congress) which makes laws.

    b. Executive Branch (the President) which enforces the laws.

    c. Judicial Branch (Courts) which interprets the laws.

31. What does "checks and balances" mean?

30. ¿En cuántas ramas se divide el gobierno de los Estados Unidos y cuál es la función de cada una?

    a. Rama Legislativa (El Congreso) que hace las leyes.

    b. Rama Ejecutiva (El Presidente) que pone en ejecución las leyes.

    c. Rama Judicial (los Tribunales) que interpretan las leyes.

31. ¿Qué quiere decir "checks and balances" (controles y equilibrios)?

"Checks and balances, quiere decir la forma en la cual las ramas del gobierno comparten el poder para que ninguna rama o persona se pueda volver demasiado poderosa y dominar a los demás.

La Rama Legislativa del Gobierno

32. ¿Cuál es el objeto de la rama Legislativa?

La rama legislativa hace las leyes.

33. ¿De qué consiste la rama Legislativa que también se conoce como el Congreso?

Hay dos "casas" en el Congreso; la Casa de los Representantes y el Senado.

34. ¿Quién hace las leyes federales de los Estados Unidos?

El Congreso hace las leyes.

35. ¿Cuáles son las calificaciones mínimas de un representante a la Casa de Representantes?

Un representante tiene que tener al menos 25 años de edad, ser ciudadano de los E.U. por 7 años al menos, y residente del estado en el cual él o ella se elige.

36. ¿Cuántos miembros tiene la Casa de Representantes?

Tiene un total de 435. El número de representantes de cada estado se basa en la población de cada estado.

37. ¿Cómo se eligen los miembros de la Casa de Representantes y cuánto duran en su puesto?

Se eligen por el pueblo en cada distrito congresional por un término de 2 años.

"Checks and balances" means the way the branches of government share power so that no one branch or person can become too powerful and dominate the others.

Principle of Checks and Balances

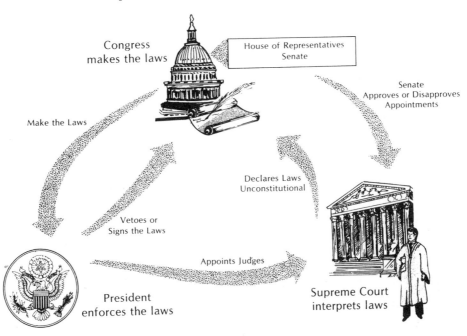

The Legislative Branch of Government

32. What is the purpose of the Legislative branch?
    The legislative branch makes the laws.
33. What makes up the Legislative branch, also known as Congress?
    There are two "houses" of Congress; the House of Representatives, and the Senate.
34. Who makes the federal laws in the United States?
    Congress makes the laws.
35. What are the minimum qualifications of a representative to the House of Representatives?
    A representative must be at least 25 years old, a U.S. citizen for at least 7 years, and a resident of the state in which he or she is elected.

38. ¿Quién preside sobre la Casa de Representantes?

   El Lider de la Casa que es escogido por los representantes preside sobre sus sesiones.

39. ¿Cuáles son las calificaciones mínimas de un Senador?

   Un senador debe de tener al menos 30 años de edad, ser ciudadano de los E.U.A. cuando menos 9 años y residente del estado del cual él o ella se elige.

40. ¿Cuántos Senadores hay?

   Hay 100 Senadores, dos de cada estado.

41. ¿Cómo se eligen los Senadores y por cuánto duran en su puesto?

   Los Senadores se eligen por voto directo del pueblo de cada estado. Duran 6 años en el puesto.

42. ¿Quién preside sobre el Senado?

   El Vice-Presidente de los Estados Unidos es el presidente del Senado y preside sobre sus sesiones.

43. ¿Por qué tiene la Casa de Representantes 435 representantes y el Senado solo tiene 100 senadores?

   Los Representantes se eligen segun el número de la gente que exista en el estado, así es que los estados que tienen una población más grande, cuentan con más representantes. En el Senado, cada estado, no importe su población tiene derecho a tener exactamente 2 senadores.

44. ¿Qué es un "Bill" (proyecto de ley)?

   Cada ley federal comienza con un "bill" el cual es una propuesta presentada por un legislador (sea un representante o un Senador) al Congreso para que se considere y se le tome alguna acción.

45. ¿Cómo se hace ley éste "bill"?

   Un "bill" se puede presentar ya sea en la casa o en el Senado. Si se aprueba en una casa, se manda a la otra. Si se vuelve a aprobar, se manda al Presidente para que él lo firme. Después de que firma el Presidente el "bill", entonces se considera una ley.

46. ¿Puede un "bill" hacerse ley sin la firma del Presidente?

   Sí, si el Presidente rehusa firmarlo (ésto se llama un veto), regresa el "bill" a la Casa, y si entonces dos terceras partes votan por él, se vuelve ley. También puede hacerse ley un "bill" si el Presidente no responde al proyecto dentro de diez días.

36. How many members are in the House of Representatives?

There are a total of 435. The number of representatives each state has is based on the population of each state.

37. How are members of the House of Representatives elected and for how long is their term of office?

They are elected by the people in each congressional district for a term of 2 years.

38. Who presides over the House of Representatives?

The Speaker of the House, who is chosen by the representatives, presides over its sessions.

39. What are the minimum qualifications of a Senator?

A Senator must be at least 30 years old, at least 9 years a citizen of the U.S.A., and a resident of the state from which he or she is elected.

40. How many Senators are there?

There are 100 Senators, two from each state.

41. How are Senators elected and for how long is their term of office?

Senators are elected by a direct vote of the people in each state. Their term of office is 6 years.

42. Who presides over the Senate?

The Vice President of the United States is President of the Senate and presides over its sessions.

43. Why does the House of Representatives have 435 representatives and the Senate only 100 Senators?

Representatives are elected according to the number of people in a state, so states with a bigger population have more representatives. In the Senate every state, regardless of population, is entitled to exactly 2 Senators.

44. What is a "bill?"

Every federal law begins as a "bill" which is a proposal submitted by a legislator (a representative or Senator) to Congress for consideration and action.

45. How does a bill become a law?

A bill may be introduced in either the House or the Senate. If passed in one house, it is sent to the other. If passed again, it is

47. ¿Cuáles son algunos de los poderes importantes del Congreso?
* declarar guerra
* proveer la acuñación de la moneda y reglamentar su valor
* recaudar y colectar los impuestos

La Rama Ejecutiva del Gobierno

48. ¿Cuál es el objeto de la rama Ejecutiva?
La rama Ejecutiva pone en ejecución las leyes.

49. ¿Quién es el ejecutivo principal?
El Presidente de los Estados Unidos es el ejecutivo principal.

50. ¿Quién fue el primer Presidente de los Estados Unidos?
George Washington tomó juramento como nuestro primer presidente en 1789.

51. ¿Cuáles son las calificaciones mínimas para el Presidente?
El Presidente de los Estados Unidos debe de tener al menos 35 años de edad, y ser residente de los Estados Unidos por al menos 14 años, y ser nacido en el país.

52. ¿Se elige el Presidente por voto del pueblo?
No directamente. El Presidente (y, el Vice-Presidente) se eligen por representantes de cada estado llamados "electores".

53. ¿Quiénes son los "electores"?
Los electores son hombres y mujeres de cada estado que votan; se les llama a estos votos, votos electorales, los electores votan a nombre de la gente de sus estados repectivos y votan por el Presidente y el Vice-Presidente.

54. ¿Cuántos electores tiene cada estado?
Cada estado tiene electores que equivalen en número al número total de los representantes y senadores que cada uno tiene.

55. ¿Cuál es el número total de los votos electorales para el Presidente y el Vice-Presidente?
Hay actualmente 538 votos electorales, 435 de la Casa de Representantes, 100 del Senado, más tres del Distrito de Colombia.

56. ¿Cuánto dura en su puesto el Presidente de los Estados Unidos?
Un presidente es elegido por un período de 4 años. La 22a

sent to the President to be signed. After the President signs the bill, it becomes a law.

46. Can a bill become a law without the President's signature?

Yes. If the President refuses to sign (this is called a "veto"), the bill must go back to the House, and if it can be passed by a two-thirds vote it becomes a law. A bill can also become a law if the President does not respond to it within ten days.

47. What are some important powers of Congress?

 * To declare war
 * To provide for coining money and to regulate its value
 * To levy and collect taxes

The Executive Branch of Government

48. What is the purpose of the Executive branch?

The Executive branch enforces the laws.

49. Who is the chief executive?

The President of the United States is the chief executive.

50. Who was the first President of the United States?

George Washington was sworn in as our first president in 1789.

51. What are the minimum qualifications for the President?

The President of the United States must be at least 35 years old, at least 14 years a resident of the United States, and native born.

52. Is the President elected by popular vote of the people?

Not directly. The President (and Vice President) are elected by representatives from each state called "electors."

53. Who are "electors?"

Electors are men and women from each state who cast votes, called electoral votes, on behalf of the people of their respective states, for the President and Vice President.

54. How many electors does each state have?

Each state has electors equal in number to the total number of representatives and senators it has.

55. What is the total number of electoral votes cast for President and Vice President?

There are currently 538 electoral votes, 435 for the House of

Presidents of the United States

PRESIDENTS OF THE UNITED STATES

President	Party	Office Term
George Washington	None	1789-1797
John Adams	Fed.	1797-1801
Thomas Jefferson	Rep.[1]	1801-1809
James Madison	Rep.[1]	1809-1817
James Monroe	Rep[1]	1817-1825
John Quincy Adams	Rep[1]	1825-1829
Andrew Jackson	Dem.	1829-1837
Martin Van Buren	Dem.	1837-1841
William Henry Harrison	Whig	1841
John Tyler	Whig	1841-1845
James K. Polk	Dem.	1845-1849
Zachary Taylor	Whig	1849-1850
Millard Fillmore	Whig	1850-1853
Franklin Pierce	Dem.	1853-1857
James Buchanan	Dem.	1857-1861
Abraham Lincoln	Rep.	1861-1865
Andrew Johnson	Rep.	1865-1869
Ulysses S. Grant	Rep.	1869-1877
Rutherford B. Hayes	Rep.	1877-1881
James A. Garfield	Rep.	1881
Chester A. Arthur	Rep.	1881-1885
Grover Cleveland	Dem.	1885-1889
Benjamin Harrison	Rep.	1889-1893
Grover Cleveland	Dem.	1893-1897
William McKinley	Rep.	1897-1901
Theodore Roosevelt	Rep.	1901-1909
William H. Taft	Rep.	1909-1913
Woodrow Wilson	Dem.	1913-1921
Warren G. Harding	Rep.	1921-1923
Calvin Coolidge	Rep.	1923-1929
Herbert C. Hoover	Rep.	1929-1933
Franklin D. Roosevelt	Dem.	1933-1945
Harry S. Truman	Dem.	1945-1953
Dwight D. Eisenhower	Rep.	1953-1961
John F. Kennedy	Dem.	1961-1963
Lyndon B. Johnson	Dem.	1963-1969
Richard M. Nixon	Rep.	1969-1974
Gerald R. Ford	Rep.	1974-1977
James Earl Carter	Dem.	1977-1981
Ronald Reagan	Rep.	1981-1989
George Bush	Rep.	1989-

[1] The party is often called the Democratic-Republican party because in the 1820's it became the Democratic party.

enmienda de la Constitucion limita el número de términos al señalar: "Ninguna persona puede ser elegida al puesto de Presidente más de dos veces..." Por lo tanto, un Presidente puede servir un máximo de 2 periodos, o sea 8 años.

57   ¿Cuándo comienza el Presidente su periodo en el cargo?

El veinte de enero, despues de la elección, el Presidente elegido toma su "Juramento Oficial". Este día se conoce como el "Día de Inauguración", y es el comienzo oficial del periodo del nuevo presidente.

58.   ¿Cuáles son algunos deberes importantes del Presidente?
* nacer cumplir las leyes federales
* ser el Comandante y Jefe de las fuerzas armadas en tiempo de guerra
* nombrar los jueces a la Suprema Corte
* nombrar a los miembros del gabinete o ministerio (los oficiales ejecutivos del Presidente)
* hacer tratados con otras naciones
* otorgarles perdones a personas convictas de crímenes en las cortes federales

59.   ¿Puede el Presidente declarar guerra?

No, solo el Congreso puede declarar guerra, pero el Presidente puede ordenarles a las tropas que comiencen acciones sin una declaración formal de guerra.

60.   ¿Se puede remover el Presidente durante su término de puesto?

Sí, a través de la impugnación, seguida por un juicio y una convicción.

61.   ¿Qué quiere decir "Impeachment" (impugnación)?

La impugnación es una acusación de grave mala conducta por un oficial del gobierno en el desempeño de sus deberes públicos.

62.   ¿Quién tiene el poder de enjuiciar a un oficial federal que sea impugnado?

Solamente el Senado puede enjuiciar un oficial del gobierno que esté acusado o impugnado.

63.   ¿Quién tiene el poder de impugnación sobre un oficial federal?

La Casa de Representantes solamente tiene el poder de impugnar (acusar).

64.   ¿Qué es el "Gabinete" (Ministerio)?

Representatives, 100 for the Senate, plus three for the District of Columbia.

56. How long is the term of office for the President of the United States?

A President is elected for a term of 4 years. The 22nd amendment to the Constitution states "No person shall be elected to the office of the President more than twice..." Therefore, a President may serve a maximum of two terms, or 8 years.

57. When does the President begin the term of office?

On January 20th, following the election, the elected President takes the "Oath of Office." This is called "Inauguration Day," and is the official beginning of the new president's term.

58. What are some important duties of the President?

* To enforce federal laws
* To be Commander-in-Chief of the armed forces in times of war
* To appoint justices of Supreme Court
* To appoint cabinet members (the President's executive officers)
* To make treaties with other nations
* To grant pardons to persons convicted of crimes in federal courts.

59. Can the President declare war?

No, only Congress can declare war, but the President can order troops into action without a formal declaration of war.

60. Can the President be removed during his or her term of office?

Yes, by impeachment, followed by trial and conviction.

61. What does "impeachment" mean?

Impeachment is an accusation of serious misconduct by a government official in the performance of his or her public duties.

62. Who has the power of impeachment of a federal official?

The House of Representatives, alone, has the power to impeach (accuse).

63. Who has the power to try an impeached official?

Only the Senate can try an accused, or impeached, federal government official.

64. What is the "Cabinet?"

El Gabinete lo forman un grupo de consejeros del Presidente. Cada funcionario del Gabinete es el jefe de uno de los departamentos ejecutivos.

65. ¿Cuáles son algunos de los jefes de departamentos que ejercen en el Gabinete?

Algunos son: el Secretario de Estado, el Secretario de la Tesorería, el Secretario de la Defensa, el Procurador General, el Secretario del Interior, el Secretario de la Acricultura, el Secretario de Transportación.

66. ¿Cómo se hace una persona miembro del Gabinete?

Los miembros del Gabinete son nombrados por el Presidente con el consentimiento del Senado.

67. ¿Quién toma el lugar del Presidente si a caso no puede terminar su período?

El Vice-Presidente tomará el cargo del Presidente en caso de la muerte del Presidente, o, si se le remueve de su puesto. Luego sigue, el Vice-Presidente, el Lider de la Casa y después de él, sigue el Presidente pro-tempore, (quiere decir "por mientras") del Senado.

68. ¿Cuántos Presidentes hemos tenido incluyendo a George Bush?

El Presidente, George Bush es el cuadragésimo primer presidente de los Estados Unidos.

La Rama Judicial Del Gobierno

69. ¿Qué objeto tiene la rama judicial?

La rama Judicial interpreta las leyes federales.

70. ¿Cuál es el tribunal más alto de los Estados Unidos?

La Corte Suprema es el Tribunal más alto de toda la tierra.

71. ¿Cuándo está en sesión la Suprema Corte?

Normalmente se reúne de octubre a junio.

72. ¿Dónde se reúne la Suprema Corte?

Se reúne en el Edificio de la Suprema Corte en Washington, D.C.

73. ¿Cuántos miembros tiene la Suprema Corte?

Tiene un total de 90 miembros. Uno de ellos el el Juez Principal, más 8 asociados, que se sientan como un grupo a oir causas y

The Cabinet is made up of a group of advisors to the President. Each Cabinet officer heads one of the executive departments.

65. What are some of these department heads who sit in the Cabinet?

Some are: Secretary of State, Secretary of the Treasury, Secretary of Defense, Attorney General, Secretary of the Interior, Secretary of Agriculture, Secretary of Transportation.

66. How does a person become a Cabinet member?

Cabinet members are appointed by the President with the consent of the Senate.

67. Who takes the President's place if he cannot finish his term of office?

The Vice President shall carry out the duties of the President upon the President's death or removal from office. Next in line after the Vice President is the Speaker of the House and after the Speaker is the President pro tempore (meaning "for the time being") of the Senate.

68. How many Presidents have we had up to and including George Bush?

President Bush became the 41st President of the United States.

The Judicial Branch of Government

69. What is the purpose of the Judicial branch?

The Judicial branch interprets the federal laws.

70. What is the highest court in the United States?

The Supreme Court is the highest court of the land.

71. When is the Supreme court in session?

It usually meets from October to June.

72. Where does the Supreme Court meet?

It meets in the Supreme Court Building in Washington, D.C.

73. How many members has the Supreme Court?

It has a total of 9 members. One of them is Chief Justice, plus 8 associates, who sit as a group, hear cases, and decide them by a majority vote of the justices.

74. How does a person become a Supreme Court justice and for how long is the term?

decidirlas por voto de la mayoriá de los jueces.

74. ¿Cómo puede hacerse una persona juez de la Corte Suprema? Por cuanto tiempo es su periodo?

Los jueces son nombrados por el Presidente por vida, pero el Senado debe de aprobar los nombramientos.

75. ¿Cuál es uno de los más importantes deberes de los jueces de la Suprema Corte?

Los jueces deciden si las leyes aprobadas por el Congreso concuerdan con la Constitución.

76. ¿Tiene el Congreso poder sobre la Suprema Corte?

Si, el Congreso determina el número de jueces y les fija su sueldo.

77. ¿Además de la Suprema Corte, hay algunas otras cortes federales?

Si, el Congreso usó su autorización recibida de la Constitución para establecer un sistema de cortes federales más bajas que consisten de, cortes del distrito y cortes de circuito.

78. ¿Quién nombra los jueces federales?

El Presidente los nombra con el consentimiento del Senado.

79. ¿Cómo se le puede remover a un juez federal de su puesto?

Un juez federal se puede remover solamente por el Congreso y al impugnarlo y encontrarlo culpable de crímenes o delitos menores igual que un oficial público.

La Guerra Entre los Estados — Guerra Civil

80. ¿Quién fué el Presidente durante la Guerra Civil?

Abraham Lincoln o, el "Honesto Abe" como lo conocían sus compatriotas, fue presidente durante la Guerra Civil. Fue el décimosexto presidente de los Estados Unidos.

81. ¿Cuándo comenzó la Guerra Civil y cuándo se terminó, y cuál fue su causa?

Comenzó en 1861 sobre el problema de la esclavitud y la doctrina de los "Derechos Estatales", que quería decir el derecho de los dueños de las plantaciones en los estados sureños de ser dueños de esclavos. La guerra se terminó en 1865.

82. ¿Cuándo y porqué se introdujo la esclavitud a la América?

The justices are appointed by the President for life, but the Senate must approve the appointments.

75. What is one of the most important duties of the Supreme Court justices?

The justices decide whether laws passed by Congress agree with the Constitution.

76. Does Congress have any power over the Supreme Court?

Yes. Congress determines the number of justices, and fixes their pay.

77. Besides the Supreme Court, are there any other Federal courts?

Yes. Congress used the authority given to it by the Constitution to establish a system of lower Federal courts, consisting of district courts and circuit courts.

78. Who appoints Federal judges?

The President appoints them with the consent of the Senate.

79. How can a Federal judge be removed from office?

A Federal judge can be removed only by Congress, by being impeached and convicted for crimes or misdemeanors as a public official.

ORGANIZATION OF FEDERAL, STATE AND CITY GOVERNMENTS			
	FEDERAL	STATE	CITY
EXECUTIVE BRANCH	President Vice President and President's Cabinet	Governor and Governor's Assistants	Mayor City Manager or City Commissioner and Assistants
LEGISLATIVE BRANCH	— Congress — House of Representatives and Senate	State Legislature Two Houses in all States except Nebraska	City Council or Commission
JUDICIAL BRANCH	Supreme Court Federal Court	State Courts	City Courts

En 1619, los mercaderes holandeses de esclavos trajeron de Africa a ésta gente y los vendieron a los primeros colonos. Los granjeros de Virginia y otras partes del Sur los deseaban como trabajadores para sus plantaciones.

83. ¿Cuál fue el resultado de la Guerra Civil?

Que se revocara la Esclavitud en 1863 con la "Proclamación de Emancipación" de Abraham Lincoln. Entonces en 1865, la Enmienda 13 se añadió a la Constitución revocando la esclavitud. Se conservó la unión de los Estados Unidos de América.

Gobiernos Estatales y Municipales

84. ¿Cómo se gobiernan los 50 estados?

Cada estado tiene su gobierno separado y se gobierna bajo su própia constitución. La constitución de un estado no puede estar en conflicto en ninguna manera con la Constitución de los Estados Unidos.

85. ¿Cuáles son algunos de los poderes de los gobiernos estatales?

* Proveer escuelas
* Proteger la vida y la propiedad
* Proveer la salubridad y el bienestar de sus ciudadanos
* Reglamentar la organización y el funcionamiento de negocios, de las corporaciones y sus condiciones de trabajo.

The War Between the States — The Civil War

80. Who was President during the Civil War?

    Abraham Lincoln or "Honest Abe," as he was known to his fellow countrymen, was President during the Civil War. He was the 16th President of the U.S.A.

81. When did the Civil War begin and end, and what was its cause?

    It began in 1861 over the issue of slavery and the doctrine of "States Rights," meaning the rights of plantation owners in Southern states to own slaves. The war ended in 1865.

82. When and why was slavery introduced in America?

    In 1619, Dutch slave traders brought people from Africa and sold them to the early colonists. The farmers in Virginia and other parts of the South wanted them for laborers on their plantations.

83. What was the result of the Civil War?

    Slavery was abolished in 1863 with Abraham Lincoln's "Emancipation Proclamation." Then in 1865, Amendment 13 was added to the Constitution abolishing slavery. The union of the United States of America was preserved.

State and City Governments

84. How are each of the 50 states governed?

    Each state has its own separate government and is governed under its own constitution. A state constitution may not in any way conflict with the Constitution of the United States.

85. What are some of the powers of the state governments?

    *   To provide schools
    *   To protect life and property
    *   To provide for the health and welfare of its citizens
    *   To regulate the organization and work of business, corporations, working conditions
    *   To make laws regarding such things as unemployment, disability insurance and workmen's compensation.

THE UNITED STATES OF AMERICA
and year each was admitted to the Union

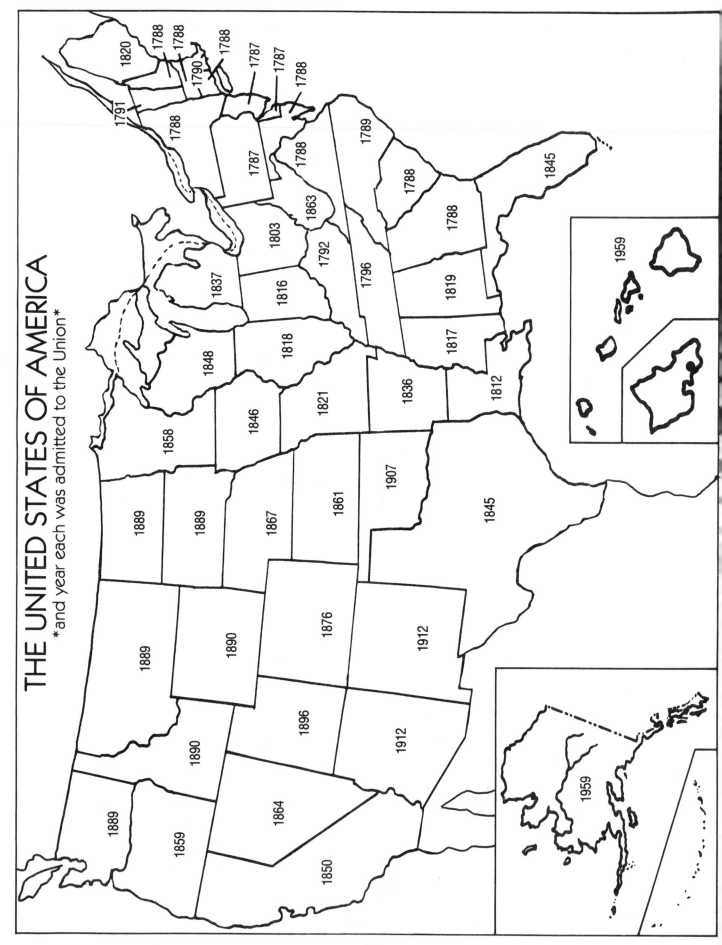

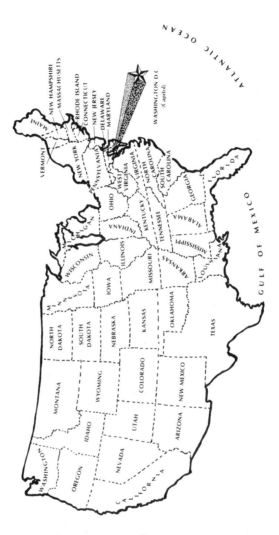

ATLANTIC OCEAN

NEW HAMPSHIRE
MASSACHUSETTS
RHODE ISLAND
CONNECTICUT
NEW JERSEY
DELAWARE
MARYLAND
WASHINGTON D.C.
(Capitol)

MAINE

VERMONT

NEW YORK

PENNSYLVANIA

WEST
VIRGINIA

VIRGINIA

NORTH
CAROLINA

SOUTH
CAROLINA

GEORGIA

OHIO

KENTUCKY

TENNESSEE

ALABAMA

FLORIDA

GULF OF MEXICO

MICHIGAN

INDIANA

ILLINOIS

WISCONSIN

MISSISSIPPI

MISSOURI

ARKANSAS

LOUISIANA

IOWA

MINNESOTA

KANSAS

OKLAHOMA

NORTH
DAKOTA

SOUTH
DAKOTA

NEBRASKA

TEXAS

MONTANA

WYOMING

COLORADO

NEW MEXICO

IDAHO

UTAH

ARIZONA

WASHINGTON

OREGON

NEVADA

CALIFORNIA

PACIFIC OCEAN

ALASKA

HAWAII

93

86. ¿Quién formó la constitución estatal de cada estado?

Se formaron por la gente de cada estado a través de sus representantes elegidos.

87. ¿Quién hace las leyes estatales?

La legislatura del estado hace las leyes.

88. ¿Cómo se eligen los legisladores estatales?

Los legisladores se eligen por voto directo del pueblo de cada estado.

89. ¿Cuál es el puesto más importante del gobierno estatal?

El gobernador es el ejecutivo principal del estado.

90. ¿Por quién y por cuánto tiempo se eligen los gobernadores?

Los gobernadores son elegidos por la gente de cada estado por un término de 4 años.

91. ¿Quién preside sobre el senado del estado?

El Teniente-gobernador preside.

92. ¿Qué otra forma de gobierno local existe?

Además de los gobiernos del condado y la ciudad, el pueblo y la villa también pueden tener una unidad de gobierno local.

93. ¿El condado es un gobierno importante local en muchos estados; el cual está a cargo del gobierno del condado?

Una Cámara de supervisores o comisionados normalmente está a cargo del gobierno del condado.

94. ¿Quién encabeza el gobierno municipal?

El alcalde o administrador municipal encabeza el gobierno municipal.

95. ¿Quién hace las leyes y los reglamentos locales de una ciudad?

El Consejo Municipal las hace.

96. ¿Cómo se llama la constitución de una ciudad y como se llaman las leyes municipales?

La constitución se llama un "charter" (la carta) y las leyes municipales se llaman "Ordinances" (reglamentos).

97. ¿De qué se tratan algunos de los reglamentos comunes?

* Reglamentos del tránsito y estacionamiento de vehículos
* La construcción de edificios
* Tirar la basura

86. Who formed the state constitution in each state?

They were formed by the people of each state through their elected representatives.

87. Who makes the state laws?

The state legislature makes laws.

88. How are state legislators elected?

The legislators are elected by direct vote of the people of each state.

89. Which is the most important office in state government?

The governor is the chief executive of the state.

90. By whom, and for how long, are governors elected?

Governors are elected by the people of each state for a term of 4 years.

91. Who presides over the state senate?

The lieutenant governor presides.

92. What other forms of local government are there?

Besides county and city governments, the town and village may also be a unit of local government.

93. The county is an important local government in most states; who is in charge of the county government?

A board of supervisors or commissioners is usually in charge of the county government.

94. Who is the head of city government?

The mayor or city manager heads city government.

95. Who makes the city's local laws and regulations?

The city council makes them.

96. What is the constitution of a city called, and what are city laws called?

The constitution is called a "charter," and the city laws are called "ordinances."

97. What are some common ordinances about?

* Vehicle traffic and parking regulations
* Construction of buildings
* Disposal of garbage

Nuestra Bandera e Himno Nacional

98. ¿Cómo se llama nuestro himno nacional?

El "Star-Spangled Banner" (La Bandera con Barras y Estrellas)

99. ¿Cuáles son los colores de la bandera de los Estados Unidos y que significan?

Los colores son: rojo, que significa el valor; blanco, que significa la verdad; y, azul, que significa la justicia.

100. ¿Cuantas franjas tiene la bandera y que significan?

Hay 7 franjas rojas y 6 franjas blancas que simbolizan los 13 estados originales.

101. ¿Cuántas estrellas tiene la bandera de los Estados Unidos?

Hay 50 estrellas, cada una representa a un estado. La primera bandera de los E.U. tenía 13 estrellas, una para cada uno de los 13 estados originales, y una estrella se añadía cada vez que otro estado se unía a los Estados Unidos.

102. Dé usted la Promesa de Fidelidad.

"Prometo fidelidad a la bandera de los Estados Unidos de América y a la República que representa, una nación, bajo Dios, indivisible, con libertad y justicia para todos".

Al conocer las respuestas de éstas 102 preguntas, leyendo la Constitución en el Apéndice 7, al revisar la fotocopia que hizo usted de su solicitud, y al sentirse agusto con el inglés, podrá usted completar con éxito el Segundo Paso: La Audiencia Preliminar.

Our Flag and Anthem

98. What is the name of our national anthem?

   The Star-Spangled Banner is our national anthem.

99. What are the colors of the United States Flag, and what do they stand for?

   The colors are **red**, which stands for courage, **white**, which stands for truth, and **blue** for justice.

100. How many stripes are on the flag, and what do they stand for?

   There are 7 red and 6 white stripes which symbolize the original 13 states.

101. How many stars are there on the United States flag?

   There are 50 stars, each **representing one state**. The first United States flag had 13 stars, one for each of the original 13 states, and one star was added each time another state joined the United States.

102. Give the Pledge of Allegiance:

   "I pledge allegiance to the flag of the United States of America, and to the Republic for which it stands, one nation under God, indivisible, with liberty and justice for all."

By knowing the answers to these 102 questions, reading the Constitution in Appendix 7, reviewing the photocopy you made of your application, and by feeling comfortable with the English language, you will be able to successfully complete Step Two: The Preliminary Examination.

Capítulo 4
LA AUDIENCIA

El último paso en el procedimiento de naturalización es la audiencia. Es un poco formal, pero breve y sencilla. Desde luego, es una ceremonia muy importante, ya que en ella toma usted su juramento de fidelidad.

La ceremonia

Untiempo después que su petición haya sido sometida, usted recibirá una notificación para que asista asu audiencia. El tiempo entre el sometimiento de su petición y recibir la notificación para que asista a la audiencia depende de qué tan seguido se lleven a cabo esas audiencias en su área. En algunas áreas las audiencias pueden ponerse una ves por semana, pero en otras pueden tener solamente dos, tres o cuatro al año.

El lugar para su audiencia puede o no ser un tribunal. Depende del juez, decidir, cómo acomodar el número de personals que se van a naturalizar en su grupo. Si el grupo es muy grande, la ceremonia puede tomar lugar en un auditorio o en un teatro. En junio de 1981, 9,700 personas fueron naturalizadas en el Coliseo de Los Angeles. No se le exige que traiga a sus hijos a la audiencia final.

La notificaciónque reciba por correo se parecerá al ejemplar 8. Un escrudiñador de naturalización, posiblemente el que condujo su audiencia preliminar, le informa al juez que usted ha sido calificado para la naturalización y debe de hacerlo ciudadano. En general, porque el en esta audiencia no se le nacen preguntas escudriñador de naturalización ya lo ha hecho. Cuando la corte decide que usted debe de ser hecho ciudadano, entonces usted toma su promesa de fidelidad a los Estados Unidos. Dice así:

Chapter 4
THE HEARING

The last step in the naturalization process is the hearing. It is somewhat formal, yet brief and simple. It is, of course, a very important ceremony, since this is where you take your oath of allegiance.

The ceremony

Some time after your petition has been filed, you will receive a notice to appear for your hearing. The length of time between filing your petition and receiving notice to appear at the hearing depends on how often these hearings are held in your area. In some areas hearings may be set as often as weekly, but other areas may have them only two, three, or four times each year.

The place of your hearing may or may not be in a courtroom. It is up to the discretion of the judge as to how to accommodate the number of people in each group to be naturalized. If the group is very large, the ceremony may be held in an auditorium or theater. In June of 1981, 9,700 persons became naturalized in the Los Angeles Coliseum. You are not required to bring your children to the final hearing.

The notification you receive in the mail will resemble Sample 8. A naturalization examiner, possibly the one who conducted your preliminary hearing, informs the judge that you have been found qualified for naturalization and should be made a citizen. Generally, you are not asked any questions at this hearing, because the naturalization examiner has already done so. When the court decides that you should be made a citizen, you take an oath of allegiance to the United States. It reads as follows:

Juramento de Fidelidad

"Con ésto declaro, bajo juramento que yo absolutamente y enteramente renuncio y descarto toda fidelidad y fe en cualquier príncipe extranjero, potentado, o estado o soberano del cual y al cual hasta ahora he sido súbdito o ciudadano; que respaldaré y defendere la Constitución de los Estados Unidos de América contra todo enemigo extranjero o doméstico; que tendré fe verdadera y fidelidad al mismo; que portaré armas a nombre de los Estados Unidos cuando se exija por ley; que prestaré servicio no de combate en las fuerzas armadas de los Estados Unidos cuando se me exija por ley; y que tomo ésta responsabilidad libremente sin reserva mental de ninguna clase o propósito de evasion, asi séa bajo pena de Dios"

Puesto más sencillamente, el juramento quiere decir:

Juro yo, que completamente renuncio a mi lealdad al país y gobierno del cual he sido hasta ahora ciudadano o sujeto. Doy toda mi lealdad y apoyo a la Constitución y a las leyes de los Estados Unidos y las obedeceré. Si me llaman, lucharé por los Estados Unidos en sus fuerzas armadas o desempeñaré todo deber que me requiera la ley. Estoy tomando ésta promesa de mi propia y libre voluntad sin intención de engañar. Asi lo juro ante Dios.

Después que se ha tomado el juramento, el juez firma la orden otorgando la naturalización y cada nuevo ciudadano recibe un Certificado de Naturalización. Este es el documento oficial que muestra que es usted ciudadano de los Estados Unidos.

El Certificado de Naturalizacion

Su Certificado de Naturalización se le dará en la audiencia, al menos que sea usted parte de un grupo muy grande que se esté

Oath of Allegiance

"I hereby declare, on oath, that I absolutely and entirely renounce and abjure all allegiance and fidelity to any foreign prince, potentate, state or sovereignty, of whom or which I have heretofore been a subject or citizen; that I will support and defend the Constitution and laws of the United States of America against all enemies, foreign and domestic; that I will bear true faith and allegiance to the same; that I will bear arms on behalf of the United States when required by law; that I will perform non-combatant service in the armed forces of the United States when required by law; that I will perform work of national importance under civilian direction when required by law; and that I take this obligation freely without any mental reservation or purpose of evasion; so help me God."

Put more simply, this is what the oath means:

I swear that I give up completely all loyalty to the country and government of which I was up to this time a citizen or a subject. I will give my full loyalty and support to the Constitution and laws of the United States, and I will obey them. If called upon, I will fight for the United States in its armed forces or perform other duties as required by law. I am taking this oath of my own free will and without intent to deceive. I swear this before God.

After the oath has been taken, the judge signs the order granting naturalization, and each new citizen is given a Certificate of Naturalization. This is the official document that shows that you are now a citizen of the United States.

The Certificate of Naturalization

Your Certificate of Naturalization will be given to you at the hearing, unless you happen to be part of a very large group being

Sample 8 - Form N-445
Notification to Appear for Final Hearing

U.S. Department of Justice

Immigration and Naturalization Service

Notice of Final
Naturalization Hearing

OMB No. 1115-0052
Approval Expires 9-30-84

Petition No. __947785__

AR# __A55 416 038__

Date __Dec. 8, 1983__

Pedro Garcia-Gonzalez
621 E. Emmett St.
Santa Ana, California   92707

You are hereby notified to appear for a hearing on your petition for naturalization before a judge of the naturalization court on __December 30, 1983__
at   300 N. Spring St., Los Angeles, California

Please report promptly at __9:30 A.__ M.

If the judge finds you qualified for naturalization, you will be sworn in as a citizen.

YOU MUST BRING WITH YOU THE ITEMS MARKED [X] BELOW:

[X] This letter, WITH ALL OF THE QUESTIONS ON THE OTHER SIDE ANSWERED IN INK OR ON A TYPEWRITER.

[X] Alien Registration Receipt Card.

[X] Reentry Permit, or Refugee Travel Document.

[X] Any Immigration documents you may have.

[ ] Your child (children): _____

[ ] Other

Proper attire should be worn in court.

If you cannot come to this hearing, return this notice immediately and state why you cannot appear. In such case, you will be sent another notice of hearing at a later date.

Form N-445
(Rev. 4-15-82)N   (SEE OTHER SIDE)

U.S. Department of Justice
Immigration and Naturalization Service

To Petitioner:

In connection with the hearing to be held on your petition for naturalization, answer each of the questions below "Yes" or "No" without giving any further explanation.

The questions refer only to what has happened after the date you appeared and filed your petition for naturalization. They do not refer to anything that happened before that date.

After you have answered every question, sign your name, give your address, and fill in the date and place of signing.

You must BRING THIS COMPLETED LETTER WITH YOU to the hearing and give it to the naturalization examiner, who will question you further on your answers.

After the date you filed your petition:

1. Have you married, or been widowed, separated, or divorced?
   (If "yes" please bring the proper document, i.e.: marriage certificate, death certificate, divorce decree, separation agreement, etc.)

   (1) Answer ___No___

2. Have you been absent from the United States?

   (2) Answer ___No___

3. Have you knowingly committed any crime or offense, for which you have not been arrested; or have you been arrested, cited, charged, indicted, convicted, fined, or imprisoned for breaking or violating any law or ordinance, including traffic violations?

   (3) Answer ___No___

4. Have you joined any organization, including the Communist Party, or become associated or connected therewith in any way?

   (4) Answer ___No___

5. Have you claimed exemption from military service?

   (5) Answer ___No___

6. Has there been any change in your willingness to bear arms on behalf of the United States; to perform non-combatant service in the armed forces of the United States; to perform work of national importance under civilian direction, if the law requires it?

   (6) Answer ___No___

7. The law provides that a petitioner for naturalization shall not be regarded as a person of good moral character who, at any time after the filing of the petition for naturalization, has advocated in polygamy or been a polygamist; received income mostly from illegal gambling; been a prostitute or procured anyone for prostitution; knowingly and for gain encouraged or helped an alien to enter the United States illegally; been an illicit trafficker in drugs or marihuana, or has been a habitual drunkard. Have you been such a person or committed any of these acts?

   (7) Answer ___No___

I certify that each of the answers shown above were made by me or at my direction, and that they are true and correct.

Signed at ___Santa Ana, California___, on ___Dec. 15, 1983___
_____(City and State)_____   _____(Date)_____

Pedro Garcia-Gonzalez
(Full Signature)

621 E. Emmett St. Santa Ana
(Full Address and ZIP Code) California
92707

naturalizando. En ese caso, los certificados se tendrían que mandar por correo a cada persona. Si usted pide un cambio de nombre con su petición de naturalización, el juez lo puede así ordenar en la audiencia y si es así, su Certificado de Naturalización se expedirá en su nuevo nombre. Cuando lo reciba, sería aconsejable hacer copia del informe que lleva y guardarlo en un lugar seguro. Es delito federal hacer fotocopia de un Certificado de Naturalización. Por ésta razón, no tenemos copia de uno apareciendo en éste libro!

Reemplazo del certificado

Si su Certificado de Naturalización se pierde, se mutila, o se destruye, o si su nombre se cambia por orden judicial o por matrimonio, usted probablemente va a querer un nuevo certificado. Puede usted solicitar uno al usar el Formulario N-565 como en el ejemplar 9. Un honorario de $50.00 se le pide. Mándelo junto con la solicitud.

El significado de la Ciudadanía de los Estados Unidos

Cuando complete usted el tercer paso, la audiencia final, y adquiera su Certificado de Naturalización, al fin será usted ciudadano de los Estados Unidos. El impacto de su nueva ciudadanía se puede mejor explicar en el siguiente mensaje del Comisionado de Inmigración y Naturalización.

El Significado de la Ciudadanía de E.U.

Ahora se ha hecho usted ciudadano de los Estados Unidos de América. Ya no es usted Inglés, Francés, Italiano, o Polaco. Tampoco es usted un Americano enlazado — Polaco-Americano, Italo-Americano. Yá no es usted sujeto de un gobierno. De hoy en adelante, es usted una parte íntegra de éste Gobierno — un hombre líbre — un ciudadano de los Estados Unidos de América.

Esta ciudadanía la cual se le ha conferido a usted solemnemente, es una cosa del espíritu, nó de la carne.

naturalized. In this case, the certificates would have to be mailed to each person. If you requested a name change on your petition for naturalization, the judge may order it at the hearing, and if so, your Certificate of Naturalization will be issued in your new name. When you get it, it is advisable to make a copy of the information on it and keep it in a safe place. It is a federal offense to make a photocopy of a Certificate of Naturalization. That is also why a copy of one does not appear in this book!

Replacement

If your Certificate of Naturalization is lost, mutilated, or destroyed, or if your name is changed by court order or marriage, you will probably want to get a new certificate. You may apply for one using Form N-565, as in Sample 9. A $50.00 fee is required to be sent along with this application.

The meaning of United States citizenship

When you complete step three, the final hearing, and acquire your Certificate of Naturalization, you will have at last become a United States citizen. The impact of your new citizenship might be best stated in the following message by the Commissioner of Immigration and Naturalization.

The Meaning of United States Citizenship

Today you have become a citizen of the United States of America. You are no longer an Englishman, a Frenchman, an Italian, a Pole. Neither are you a hyphenated American — a Polish-American, an Italian-American. You are no longer a subject of a government. Henceforth, you are an integral part of this Government — a freeman — a citizen of the United States of America.

This citizenship, which has been solemnly conferred on you, is a thing of the spirit — not of the flesh. When you

Cuando usted dió su Promesa de Fidelidad a la Constitución de los Estados Unidos, reclamó por sí mismo los derechos inalienables que se asientan en ese documento sagrado como los derechos naturales de todos los hombres.

Usted ha hecho sacrificios para llegar a este fin deseado. Nosotros, sus ciudadanos compatriotas, lo reconocemos, y el calor con el cual le damos la bienvenida se aumenta proporcionalmente. Sin embargo, queremos tintarlo con una advertencia amistosa.

Como ha aprendido durante estos años de su preparación, este gran honor lleva la obligación que tiene usted de luchar por, y asegurar éste estado civil tan anhelado y el que usted ha buscado con tanto ánimo. El Gobierno bajo nuestra constitución hace la ciudadanía Americana el previlegio más alto y al mismo tiempo la responsabilidad más grande de cualquier ciudadanía del Mundo.

Los derechos importantes que goza usted ahora y los deberes y las reponsabilidades que lo acompañan se asientan en otra parte de este librillo de recuerdo. Esperamos que le servirán como un recuerdo constante de que solo al continuar sus estudios, y aprender más de su nuevo país, sus ideales, sus hazañas y sus objetivos, y, al trabajar siempre mejorando su ciudadanía puede disfrutar sus frutos y asegurar su preservación para las generaciones que vienen.

Que pueda usted encontrar en esta Nación el cumplimiento de sus sueños de paz y seguridad, y que la América en su turno no lo encuentre faltando en su nuevo y orgulloso papel de Ciudadano de los Estados dos Unidos.

took the oath of allegiance to the Constitution of the United States you claimed for yourself the God-given unalienable rights which that sacred document sets forth as the natural right of all men.

You have made sacrifices to reach this desired goal. We, your fellow citizens, realize this, and the warmth of our welcome to you is increased proportionately. However, we would tincture it with friendly caution.

As you have learned during these years of preparation, this great honor carries with it the duty to work for and make secure this longed-for and eagerly-sought status. Government under our Constitution makes American citizenship the highest privilege and at the same time the greatest responsibility of any citizenship in the world.

The important rights that are now yours and the duties and responsibilities attendant thereon are set forth elsewhere in this souvenir booklet. It is hoped that they will serve as a constant reminder that only by continuing to study and learn about your new country, its ideals, achievements, and goals, and by everlastingly working at your citizenship can you enjoy its fruits and assure their preservation for generations to follow.

May you find in this Nation the fulfillment of your dreams of peace and security, and may America, in turn, never find you wanting in your new and proud role of citizen of the United States.

Sample 9 Form N-565
Application for a New Naturalization or Citizenship Paper

U.S. Department of Justice
Immigration and Naturalization Service

OMB #1115-0015
Application for Replacement
Naturalization/Citizenship Document

START HERE - Please Type or Print

	FOR INS USE ONLY

Part 1. Information about you.

Family Name	Brand	Given Name	John	Middle Initial	W.

Address - In care of: John W. Brand

Street # and Name	1121 Avenida del Vista	Apt #

City or town	Corona	State or Province	California

Country	U. S. A.	Zip or Postal Code	91720

Date of Birth (month/day/year)	May 17, 1926	Country of Birth	Netherlands

Certificate #	Unknown	A #	Unknown

FOR INS USE ONLY

Returned

Receipt

Resubmitted

Reloc Sent

Reloc Rec'd

☐ Applicant Interviewed

Part 2. Type of application.

1. I hereby apply for: (check one)

a. ☐ a new Certificate of Citizenship

b. ☒ a new Certificate of Naturalization

c. ☐ a new Certificate of Repatriation

d. ☐ a new Declaration of Intention

e. ☐ a special Certificate of Naturalization to obtain recognition of my U.S. citizenship by a foreign country

2. Basis for application: (If you checked other than "e" in Part 1, check one)

a. ☒ my certificate was lost, stolen or destroyed (attach a copy of the certificate if you have one)

b. ☐ my certificate is mutilated (attach the certificate)

c. ☐ my name has been changed (attach the certificate)

d. ☐ my certificate or declaration is incorrect (attach the document)

☐ Declaration of Intention verified by _____

☐ Citizenship verified by _____

Remarks

Part 3. Processing information.

SEX	☒ Male ☐ Female	Height	5'10"	Marital Status	☐ Single ☒ Married	☐ Widowed ☐ Divorced

My last certificate or declaration of intention was issued to me by:

INS Office or Name of court	District Court,Los Angeles	Date (month/day/year)	Feb. 3, 1978

Since becoming a citizen, have you lost your citizenship in any manner?

☒ No   ☐ Yes (attach an explanation)

Action Block

Part 4. Complete if applying for a new document because of name change.

Name changed to present name by: (check one)   Not applicable

☐ Marriage or Divorce on (month/day/year)_____ (attach a copy of marriage or divorce certificate)

☐ Court Decree (month/day/year)_____(attach a copy of the court decree)

To Be Completed by
Attorney or Representative, if any

☐ Fill in box if G-28 is attached to represent the applicant

VOLAG#

ATTY State License #

Form N-565 (Rev. 07/02/91) N   *Continued on back.*

Part 5. **Complete if applying to correct your document.**

If you are applying for a new certificate or declaration of intention because your current one is incorrect, explain why it is incorrect and attach copies of the documents supporting your request.

Not applicable

Part 6. **Complete if applying for a special certificate of recognition as a citizen of the U.S. by the Government of the foreign country.**

Name of Foreign Country ___ Not applicable

Information about official of the country who has requested this certificate (if known)

Name   Official title

Government Agency

Address: Street # and Name		Room #
City	State or Province	
Country	Zip or Postal Code	

Part 7. **Signature.** *Read the information on penalties in the instructions before completing this part. If you are going to file this application at an INS office in the U.S., sign below. If you are going to file it at a U.S. INS office overseas, sign in front of a U.S. INS or consular official.*

I certify, or, if outside the United States, I swear or affirm, under penalty of perjury under the laws of the United States of America that this application, and the evidence submitted with it, is all true and correct. I authorize the release of any information from my records which the Immigration and Naturalization Service needs to determine eligibility for the benefit I am seeking.

Signature		Date
John William Brand	Print Name	7/18/91
Signature of INS or Consular Official		Date

Please Note: *If you do not completely fill out this form, or fail to submit required documents listed in the instructions, you may not be found eligible for a certificate and this application may be denied.*

Part 8. **Signature of person preparing form if other than above.** *(sign below)*

I declare that I prepared this application at the request of the above person and it is based on all information of which I have knowledge.

Signature	Print Your Name	Date

Firm Name and Address

*U.S. Government Printing Office: 1991 — 282-065/44287

109

M-384
8-84

Passport Services

BUREAU OF CONSULAR AFFAIRS
U.S. DEPARTMENT OF STATE
WASHINGTON, D.C. 20524

NOTICE TO NEWLY NATURALIZED CITIZENS REGARDING PASSPORTS

The Office of Passport Services of the Department of State congratulates you on your newly acquired United States citizenship.

One privilege your citizenship entitles you to is a United States passport. The passport is an official document attesting to your citizenship and identifying you for purposes of international travel. It is also official evidence that you are entitled to the protection of the United States Government while you are abroad.

Many naturalized citizens frequently travel abroad to visit relatives and the land of their birth. There have been some unfortunate instances, however, in which citizens were not able to complete emergency travel of a business or family nature because there was not sufficient time to obtain a United States passport. If you are planning to travel therefore, the Office of Passport Services urges you to apply for and maintain a valid passport at all times.

Applying for your first passport is easy, requiring only a completed application, your naturalization certificate, two recent identical photographs, and appropriate fees. All passport requirements are detailed in the brochure, "Your Trip Abroad," available at many Federal and State courts and post offices and at the passport agencies listed on the back of this notice.

Once you have a United States passport, keep it in a safe place where you can get at it quickly when you need it. The loss of a passport is a very serious matter which may cause you difficulties. Avoid this problem by safeguarding your passport as you would any valuable possession.

United States Passport Agencies

Boston Passport Agency
Suite E123
John F. Kennedy Building
Government Center
Boston, MA 02203

Chicago Passport Agency
Suite 380
Kluczynski Federal Building
230 So. Dearborn Street
Chicago, IL 60604

Honolulu Passport Agency
Suite C-106
New Federal Building
300 Ala Moana Boulevard
Honolulu, HI 96850

Houston Passport Agency
One Allen Center
500 Dallas Street
Houston, TX 77002

Los Angeles Passport Agency
Suite 13100
Federal Building
11000 Wilshire Boulevard
Los Angeles, CA 90024

Miami Passport Agency
Room 1616
Federal Office Building
51 S.W. First Avenue
Miami, FL 33130

New Orleans Passport Agency
Room T-12005
Postal Service Building
701 Loyola Avenue
New Orleans, LA 70113

New York Passport Agency
Northeast Passport Center
P. O. Box 22
New York, NY 10014

Philadelphia Passport Agency
Room 4426
Federal Building
600 Arch Street
Philadelphia, PA 19106

San Francisco Passport Agency
Suite 200
525 Market Street
San Francisco, CA 94105

Seattle Passport Agency
Suite 992
Federal Building
915 Second Avenue
Seattle, WA 98174

Washington Passport Agency
1425 K Street N.W.
Washington, DC 20524

Sample 10
Passport Application

UNITED STATES DEPARTMENT OF STATE

APPLICATION FOR ☐ PASSPORT ☐ REGISTRATION

SEE INSTRUCTIONS—TYPE OR PRINT IN INK IN WHITE AREAS

1. NAME FIRST NAME   MIDDLE NAME

LAST NAME

2. MAILING ADDRESS

STREET

CITY, STATE,
ZIP CODE

COUNTRY   IN CARE OF

☐ 5 Yr. ☐ 10 Yr.   Issue
Date _____
R   D   O   DP
End. # _____   Exp. _____

3. SEX   **4. PLACE OF BIRTH** City, State or Province, Country   **5. DATE OF BIRTH**   **6. SEE FEDERAL TAX** SOCIAL SECURITY NUMBER

Male Female   Mo. Day Year   LAW NOTICE ON REVERSE SIDE

7. HEIGHT   **8. COLOR OF HAIR**   **9. COLOR OF EYES**   **10. (Area Code) HOME PHONE**   **11. (Area Code) BUSINESS PHONE**

Feet Inches   **12. PERMANENT ADDRESS (Street, City, State, ZIP Code)**   **13. OCCUPATION**

FOLD

14. FATHER'S NAME   BIRTHPLACE   BIRTH DATE   U.S. CITIZEN   **16. TRAVEL PLANS** (Not Mandatory)
☐ YES ☐ NO   COUNTRIES   DEPARTURE DATE

15. MOTHER'S MAIDEN NAME   BIRTHPLACE   BIRTH DATE   U.S. CITIZEN   LENGTH OF STAY
☐ YES ☐ NO

17. HAVE YOU EVER BEEN ISSUED A U.S. PASSPORT?   YES ☐   NO ☐   IF YES, SUBMIT PASSPORT IF AVAILABLE.   ☐ Submitted

IF UNABLE TO SUBMIT MOST RECENT PASSPORT, STATE ITS DISPOSITION: COMPLETE NEXT LINE

NAME IN WHICH ISSUED   PASSPORT NUMBER   ISSUE DATE (Mo., Day, Yr.)   DISPOSITION

SUBMIT TWO RECENT IDENTICAL PHOTOS

2" × 2"   FROM 1" TO 1-3/8"

18. HAVE YOU EVER BEEN MARRIED? ☐ YES   ☐ NO   DATE OF MOST RECENT MARRIAGE   Mo. Day Year

WIDOWED/DIVORCED?   ☐ YES   ☐ NO   IF YES, GIVE DATE   Mo. Day Year

SPOUSE'S FULL BIRTH NAME   SPOUSE'S BIRTHPLACE

19. IN CASE OF EMERGENCY, NOTIFY (Person Not Traveling With You)   RELATIONSHIP
(Not Mandatory)
FULL NAME

ADDRESS   (Area Code) PHONE NUMBER

20. TO BE COMPLETED BY AN APPLICANT WHO BECAME A CITIZEN THROUGH NATURALIZATION

I IMMIGRATED TO THE U.S.   I RESIDED CONTINUOUSLY IN THE U.S.   DATE NATURALIZED (Mo., Day, Yr.)
(Month, Year)   From (Mo., Yr.)   To (Mo., Yr.)
PLACE

FOLD

21. DO NOT SIGN APPLICATION UNTIL REQUESTED TO DO SO BY PERSON ADMINISTERING OATH

I have not, since acquiring United States citizenship, performed any of the acts listed under "Acts or Conditions" on the reverse of this application form (unless explanatory statement is attached). I solemnly swear (or affirm) that the statements made on this application are true and the photograph attached is a true likeness of me.

Subscribed and sworn to (affirmed) before me   (SEAL)   X

Month Day Year

☐ Clerk of Court or
☐ PASSPORT Agent
☐ Postal Employee   (Sign in presence of person authorized to accept application)
☐ (Vice) Consul USA At _____

(Signature of person authorized to accept application)

22. APPLICANT'S IDENTIFYING DOCUMENTS ☐ PASSPORT ☐ DRIVER'S LICENSE ☐ OTHER (Specify)
ISSUE DATE   EXPIRATION DATE   No.
Month Day Year   Month Day Year   PLACE OF ISSUE   ISSUED IN THE NAME OF

23. FOR ISSUING OFFICE USE ONLY (Applicant's evidence of citizenship)

☐ Birth Cert.   SR   CR   City   Filed/Issued:
☐ Passport   Bearer's Name:
☐ Report of Birth
☐ Naturalization/Citizenship Cert.   No.:
☐ Other:
☐ Seen & Returned
☐ Attached

APPLICATION APPROVAL

Examiner Name

Office, Date

24.

FEE _____ EXEC. _____ POST _____

FORM DSP-11 (12-87)   (SEE INSTRUCTIONS ON REVERSE)   Form Approved OMB No. 1405-0004 (Exp. 8/1/89)

UNITED STATES DEPARTMENT OF STATE

PASSPORT APPLICATION

FEDERAL TAX LAW:

Section 6039E of the Internal Revenue Code of 1986 requires a passport applicant to provide his/her name (#1), mailing address (#2), date of birth (#5), and social security number (#6). If you have not been issued a social security number, enter zeroes in box #6. Passport Services will provide this information to the Internal Revenue Service routinely. Any applicant who fails to provide the required information is subject to a $500 penalty enforced by the IRS. All questions on this matter should be referred to the nearest IRS office.

ACTS OR CONDITIONS

(If any of the below-mentioned acts or conditions has been performed by or applies to the applicant, the portion which applies should be lined out, and a supplementary explanatory statement under oath (or affirmation) by the applicant should be attached and made a part of this application.)

I have not, since acquiring United States citizenship, been naturalized as a citizen of a foreign state; taken an oath or made an affirmation or other formal declaration of allegiance to a foreign state; entered or served in the armed forces of a foreign state; accepted or performed the duties of any office, post, or employment under the government of a foreign state or political subdivision thereof; made a formal renunciation of nationality either in the United States or before a diplomatic or consular officer of the United States in a foreign state; or been convicted by a court or court martial of competent jurisdiction of committing any act of treason against, or attempting by force to overthrow, or bearing arms against, the United States, or conspiring to overthrow, put down, or to destroy by force, the Government of the United States; or having been naturalized, within one year after such naturalization, returned to the country of my birth or any other foreign country to take up a permanent residence.

WARNING: False statements made knowingly and willfully in passport applications or in affidavits or other supporting documents submitted therewith are punishable by fine and/or imprisonment under provisions of 18 USC 1001 and/or 18 USC 1542. Alteration or mutilation of a passport issued pursuant to this application is punishable by fine and/or imprisonment under the provisions of 18 USC 1543. The use of a passport in violation of the restrictions contained therein or of the passport regulations is punishable by fine and/or imprisonment under 18 USC 1544. All statements and documents submitted are subject to verification.

PRIVACY ACT STATEMENT:

The information solicited on this form is authorized by, but not limited to, those statutes codified in Titles 8, 18, and 22, United States Code, and all predecessor statutes whether or not codified, and all regulations issued pursuant to Executive Order 11295 of August 5, 1966. The primary purpose for soliciting the information is to establish citizenship, identity, and entitlement to issuance of a United States Passport or related facility, and to properly administer and enforce the laws pertaining thereto.

The information is made available as a routine use on a need-to-know basis to personnel of the Department of State and other government agencies having statutory or other lawful authority to maintain such information in the performance of their official duties; pursuant to a court order; and, as set forth in Part 171, Title 22, Code of Federal Regulations (see *Federal Register*, Volume 42, pages 49791 through 49795).

Failure to provide the information requested on this form may result in the denial of a United States Passport, related document, or service to the individual seeking such passport, document, or service.

HOW TO APPLY FOR A U.S. PASSPORT. U.S. passports are issued only to U.S. citizens or nationals. Each person must obtain his or her own passport.

IF YOU ARE A FIRST-TIME APPLICANT, please complete and submit this application in person. (Applicants under 13 years of age usually need not appear in person unless requested. A parent or guardian may execute the application on the child's behalf.) Each application must be accompanied by (1) PROOF OF U.S. CITIZENSHIP, (2) PROOF OF IDENTITY, (3) TWO PHOTOGRAPHS, (4) FEES (as explained below) to one of the following acceptance agents: a clerk of any Federal or State court of record or a judge or clerk of any probate court accepting applications; a designated postal employee at a selected post office; or an agent at a Passport Agency in Boston, Chicago, Honolulu, Houston, Los Angeles, Miami, New Orleans, New York, Philadelphia, San Francisco, Seattle, Stamford, or Washington, D.C.; or a U.S. consular official.

IF YOU HAVE HAD A PREVIOUS PASSPORT, inquire about eligibility to use Form DSP-82 (mail-in application).

Address requests for passport amendment, extension of validity, or additional visa pages to a Passport Agency or a U.S. Consulate or Embassy abroad. Check visa requirements with consular officials of countries to be visited well in advance of your departure.

(1) PROOF OF U.S. CITIZENSHIP.

(a) APPLICANTS BORN IN THE UNITED STATES. Submit previous U.S. passport or **certified** birth certificate. A birth certificate must include your given name and surname, date and place of birth, date the birth record was filed, and seal or other certification of the official custodian of such records. A record filed more than 1 year after the birth is acceptable if it is supported by evidence described in the next paragraph.

IF NO BIRTH RECORD EXISTS, submit registrar's notice to that effect. Also submit an early baptismal or circumcision certificate, hospital birth record, early census, school, or family Bible records, newspaper or insurance files, or notarized affidavits of persons having knowledge of your birth (preferably with at least one record listed above). Evidence should include your given name and surname, date and place of birth, and seal or other certification of office (if customary) and signature of issuing official.

(b) APPLICANTS BORN OUTSIDE THE UNITED STATES. Submit previous U.S. passport or Certificate of Naturalization, or Certificate of Citizenship, or a Report of Birth Abroad, or evidence described below.

IF YOU CLAIM CITIZENSHIP THROUGH NATURALIZATION OF PARENT(S), submit the Certificate(s) of Naturalization of your parent(s), your foreign birth certificate, and proof of your admission to the United States for permanent residence.

IF YOU CLAIM CITIZENSHIP THROUGH BIRTH ABROAD TO U.S. CITIZEN PARENT(S), submit a Consular Report of Birth (Form FS-240) or Certification of Birth (Form DS-1350 or FS-545), or your foreign birth certificate, parents' marriage certificate, proof of citizenship of your parent(s), and affidavit of U.S. citizen parent(s) showing all periods and places of residence/physical presence in the United States and abroad before your birth.

(2) PROOF OF IDENTITY. If you are not personally known to the acceptance agent, you must establish your identity to the agent's satisfaction. You may submit items such as the following containing your signature AND physical description or photograph that is a good likeness of you: previous U.S. passport; Certificate of Naturalization or of Citizenship; driver's license (not temporary or learner's license); or government (Federal, State, municipal) identification card or pass. Temporary or altered documents are not acceptable.

IF YOU CANNOT PROVE YOUR IDENTITY as stated above, you must appear with an IDENTIFYING WITNESS who is a U.S. citizen or permanent resident alien who has known you for at least 2 years. Your witness must prove his or her identity and complete and sign an Affidavit of Identifying Witness (Form DSP-71) before the acceptance agent. You must also submit some identification of your own.

(3) TWO PHOTOGRAPHS. Submit two identical photographs of you alone, sufficiently recent to be a good likeness (normally taken within the last 6 months), 2 × 2 inches in size, with an image size from bottom of chin to top of head (including hair) of between 1 and 1-3/8 inches. Photographs must be clear, front view, full face, taken in normal street attire without a hat or dark glasses, and printed on thin paper with a plain light (white or off-white) background. They may be black and white or color. They must be capable of withstanding a mounting temperature of 225° Fahrenheit (107° Celsius). Photographs retouched so that your appearance is changed are unacceptable. Snapshots, most vending machine prints, and magazine or full-length photographs are unacceptable.

(4) FEES. Submit $42 if you are 18 years of age or older. The passport fee is $35. In addition, a fee of $7 is charged for the execution of the application. Your passport will be valid for 10 years from the date of issue except where limited by the Secretary of State to a shorter period. Submit $27 if you are under 18 years of age. The passport fee is $20 and the execution fee is $7. Your passport will be valid for 5 years from the date of issue, except where limited as above.

Pay the passport and execution fees in one of the following forms: checks—personal, certified, traveler's; bank draft or cashier's check; money order, U.S. Postal, international, currency exchange; or if abroad, the foreign currency equivalent, or a check drawn on a U.S. bank.

Make passport and execution fees payable to Passport Services (except if applying at a State court, pay execution fee as the State court requires) or the appropriate Embassy or Consulate, if abroad. No fee is charged to applicants with U.S. Government or military authorization for no-fee passports (except State courts may collect the execution fee). Pay special postage if applicable.

FORM DSP-11
12-87

Capítulo 5
¡AL FIN - LA CIUDADANIA ESTADOUNIDENSE!

Ya que se haga ciudadano, puede usted disfrutar de los beneficios de la ciudadanía de E.U. Estos se le escribieron en la lista del primer capítulo de éste libro bajo, "Cuáles son los Beneficios?". Un beneficio importante es la calificafición para pasaporte de E.U. Puede usted referirse al ejemplar 10, para ver la Solicitud de Pasaporte, y el Informe para los Solicitantes de Pasaporte. También, antes al ejemplar 10 es una carta de información para pasaporte y una lista de agencias de pasaportes en E.U. Es importante darse cuenta de que junto con éste beneficio y todos los demás beneficios de la ciudadanía, tambien recibe usted responsabilidades.

Contribuyendo tu parte

Un poder grande de nuestra democracia en América es que, se se preocupa por cada ciudadano individual. Cada uno de nosotros tenemos derechos y previlegios garantizados por nuestra Constitución. Cada persona comparte nuestro gobierno. Su "parte" en el gobierno de los Estados Unidos puede bien ser la respuesta a estas palabras famosas, "...no preguntes qué es lo que tu país puede hacer por ti-pregunta qué es lo que tú puedes hacer por tu país". El ex-presidente, John F. Kennedy dijo ésto en el discurso de su inauguración.

Votar:

Algo que puede usted hacer por su país es votar. Es un deber sumamente importante. Cada ciudadano está en libertad de votar en balota secreta por el candidato que quiera escoger. Esta es la forma que tenemos para conservar la democracia de nuestro gobierno bajo el cual vivimos. Franklin D. Roosevelt, otro ex-presidente, una vez dijo que la única forma de garantizar nuestra libertad es teniendo un gobierno

Chapter 5
UNITED STATES CITIZENSHIP AT LAST!

Once you become a citizen, you can enjoy all the benefits of U.S. citizenship. These were listed in Chapter 1 of this book under "What are the Benefits?" One important benefit is qualification for a U.S. passport. You may wish to refer to Sample 10 to see the Passport Application and "Information for Passport Applicants." Also, before Sample 10 is an informative letter about passports and a list of U.S. passport agencies. It is important to realize that along with this benefit and all the other benefits of citizenship you get responsibilities, too.

Doing your share

One great strength of our democracy in America is its concern for each individual citizen. Each one of us has rights and privileges guaranteed by our Constitution. Each has a share in the government. Your "share" in the United States government might well be the answer to those famous words, "...ask not what your country can do for you — ask what you can do for your country." Former President John F. Kennedy said that at his inauguration.

Voting:

Something you can do for your country is to vote. It is an extremely important duty. Each citizen is free to vote by secret ballot for the candidate of his or her choice. It is the way we preserve the democratic form of government under which we live. Franklin D. Roosevelt, another former President, once said that the only way to guarantee our liberty is to have a government strong enough to protect the interests of all the people, and to have the people strong enough and well enough informed to maintain control over their government. One way for you to exert some control is to vote. It could be your one vote that makes a big difference. Did you know that:

In 1645: ONE VOTE gave Oliver Cromwell control of England.

suficientemente poderoso para proteger los intereses de toda la gente, y teniendo un pueblo suficientemente fuerte y bien informado para mantener el control de su gobierno. Una forma para que usted pueda ejercer algun control, es, con el voto. Puede ser el voto suyo el que haga toda la diferencia. Sabía usted que:

En 1645 - UN VOTO le dió a Oliver Cromwell contról de Inglaterra

En 1649 - UN VOTO causó la ejecución de Carlos I de Inglaterra.

En 1776 - UN VOTO le dió a América el idioma inglés en vez del alemán.

En 1839 - UN VOTO eligió a Marcus Morton como gobernador de Massachusetts.

En 1876 - UN VOTO salvó al Presidente Andrew Johnson de impugnación.

En 1876 - UN VOTO cambió a Francia de la monarquía a una república.

En 1923 - UN VOTO le dio a Adolfo Hitler su Jefatura del Partido Nazi.

¡Cada Voto Sí Cuenta!

Empadronándose Para Votar:

Para votar, usted tiene que registrarse en la comunidad adonde vive. Registrarse es un procedimiento sencillo. Solo necesita llenar una tarjeta como la que se vé en el ejemplar 11, "Tarjeta de Registro del Votante". Se puede hacer por correo o en persona. Telefonée o vaya a la oficina de Registro de Votantes en su edificio del condado local o el palacio municipal de su localidad. Tales tarjetas pueden ser un poco diferentes de comunidad a comunidad, pero básicamente, todas requieren la misma información. Dése cuenta que usted debe de marcar su afiliación de "partido político", que es al cual usted pertenece o en el cual usted tiene fe. Si no lo sabe o si no quiere usted que sepa nadie, esté seguro de marcar adonde dice, "Rehuso declararlo". Es su previlegio así hacerlo. Sólo no deje nada en blanco. Marque algo o puede que su tarjeta se le considere incompleta, y que no lo registren. Empadrónese para votar bastante tiempo antes de una elección, ya que hay ciertos límites de

In 1645: ONE VOTE gave Oliver Cromwell control of England.

In 1649: ONE VOTE caused Charles I of England to be executed.

In 1776: ONE VOTE gave America the English language instead of German.

In 1839: ONE VOTE elected Marcus Morton Governor of Massachusetts.

In 1876: ONE VOTE saved President Andrew Johnson from impeachment.

In 1876: ONE VOTE changed France from a monarchy to a republic.

In 1923: ONE VOTE gave Adolph Hitler leadership of the Nazi Party.

Every vote does count!

Registering to vote:

In order to vote, you must first register in the community where you live. Registration is a very simple process. You need only fill out a card like the one in Sample 11, "Voter Registration Card." It can be done by mail or in person. Either phone or go to the Voter Registration

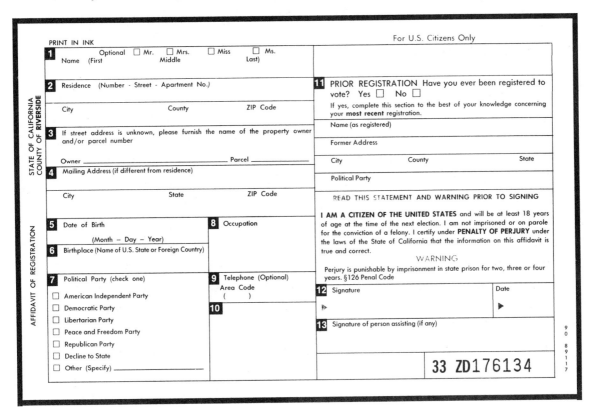

tiempo. Es buena idea que se empadrone tan pronto como se haga usted ciudadano, y cada vez que se mude, tiene que hacerlo todo de nuevo otra vez. Por supuesto, para votar, los ciudadanos deben tener al menos 18 años de edad, según la Enmienda 26 de nuestra Constitución. El registrarse para votar solo toma unos pocos minutos, y no puede votar usted al menos que se registre.

Regístrese e infórmese bien. Aprenda algo sobre los candidatos que se postulan. Mire las noticias de la televisión, y lea los periódicos y revistas al menos. Entonces, decida usted quién piensa que es el candidato mejor calificado. El día de la elección, salga usted a votar!

El Estar Bien Informado:

Además de votar, su "parte" en el gobierno incluye el ser un ciudadano bien informado. Conozca lo que esté sucediendo en su comunidad, en la nación y alrededor del mundo. Se les puede confiar su propio gobierno a las personas bien informadas. Thomas Jefferson, el tercer presidente de nuestro país una vez escribió:

"...cuando las cosas llegan al punto de estar tan mal encarriladas, puede uno contar con que la gente, si es que está bien informada, las arreglará."

Usted puede expresar su opinión al escribirle a su representante del Congreso o al editor de su periódico local. Su opinión, si está bien informada, es una que se basa sobre los hechos.

Además de votar y de ser un ciudadano bien informado, nuestra "parte" incluye el ser leal y tener la buena gana de defender a los E.U.. Debemos de respetar los derechos de otros, obedecer las leyes, y sí, tambien pagar impuestos a cambio de los servicios que recibimos del gobierno. Mucho todavía se tiene que hacer para crear una vida buena para todos en los Estados Unidos. El éxito continuado o el fracaso de esta gran nación queda en las manos de sus ciudadanos. Esta, entoces, es nuestra "parte", nuestro deber, nuestro previlegio.

done by mail or in person. Either phone or go to the Voter Registration office in your local county building or city hall. Such cards may differ slightly from community to community, but basically, they all require the same information. Notice that you are to check your "political party" affiliation, the one you belong to or believe in. If you don't know or don't want anyone else to know, be sure to check "Decline to state." It is your privilege to do so. Just don't leave any blanks. Check something or else your card may be considered incomplete, and you won't be registered. Register to vote well in advance of an election, as there are time limits. It's a good idea to register as soon as you become a citizen, and every time you move, you must do so all over again. Of course, in order to vote, citizens must be at least 18 years old according to Amendment 26 of our Constitution. Registering to vote just takes a few minutes, and you can't vote unless you register.

Register and become informed. Learn about the candidates who are running for office. Watch television newscasts and read the newspapers and magazines, at least. Then, decide who you think is the best qualified candidate. On election day, get out and vote!

Being informed:

Besides voting, your "share" in the government includes being a well-informed citizen. Know what is going on in your community, in the nation, and around the world. People who are well-informed can be trusted with their own government. Thomas Jefferson, our country's third President, once wrote:

> "...whenever things get so far wrong as to attract
> their notice, the people, if well informed, may be
> relied on to set them to rights."

You can express your opinion by writing your Congressman or the editor of a local newspaper. Your opinion, if well-informed, is one that is based on facts.

In addition to voting and being informed citizens, our "share" includes being loyal and willing to defend the U.S.A. We must respect

Conocer a Nuestra America

Hacer cosas tal como el guardar las fiestas tradicionales nacionales y el recitar nuestra Promesa de Fidelidad en la escuela son sólo dos maneras en las cuales usted puede hacerse parte de las costumbres americanas. Lea las páginas que siguen y familiarícese con algunas canciones, símbolos y días de fiesta de nuestro país.

Las Cinco Cualidades de un Buen Ciudadano*

El Buen Ciudadano aprecia los valores democráticos y basa sus acciones sobre ellos.

El buen ciudadano da su fidelidad a los ideales de la democracia. Aprecia los valores que concuerdan con la costumbre democrática de vivir y, vive en el espíritu de estos valores. Tiene respeto por la dignidad y el valor de la personalidad humana. Tiene fe en la capacidad del hombre para resolver los problemas comunes a través del procedimiento del pensamiento. Se mortifica por el bienestar general de toda la gente; tiene fe que la cultura humana le pertenece a todos los hombres. Es leal a los principios de la igualdad de las oportunidades para todos. Todas las características del ciudadano bueno vienen de, y son parte de esta calidad primaria.

El Buen Ciudadano practica las relaciones democráticas humanas en su familia, en la escuela, en la comunidad, y en otros foros más grandes.

El buen ciudadano reconoce la interdependencia de toda la gente en su familia, escuela, comunidad, y las relaciones nacionales y mundiales. Practica las clases de relaciones humanas que concuerdan con la sociedad democrática. Toma a pecho lo que les sucede a otros, así gana el respeto y la confianza. Desarrolla su propia capacidad de cooperar con otros. Sinceramente desea

the rights of others, obey the laws, and yes, pay taxes in return for the services we receive from government. Much remains to be done in order to create a good life for all in the United States. The continued success, or the failure, of this great nation rests in the hands of all its citizens. This, then, is our "share," our duty, our privilege.

Knowing our America

Doing things like observing traditional national holidays and reciting the Pledge of Allegiance at school are just two ways in which you can become a part of the American way of life. Browse through the following pages and familiarize yourself with some songs, symbols, and holidays of our country.

The Five Qualities Of The Good Citizen*

The Good Citizen cherishes democratic values and bases his actions on them.

> The good citizen gives allegiance to the ideals of democracy. He cherishes values which are consistent with the democratic way of life and lives in the spirit of these values. He has respect for the dignity and worth of human personality. He has faith in man's ability to solve common problems through the process of thinking. He is concerned with the general welfare of all people; he believes that human culture belongs to all men. He is loyal to the principles of equality of opportunity for all. All other characteristics of the good citizen stem from, and are a part of this primary quality.

The Good Citizen practices democratic human relationship in the family, school, community, and the larger scenes.

> The good citizen recognizes the interdependence of all people in family, school, community, national, and

121

ayudar a otros. A través de éstas prácticas, edifica la buena voluntad como un recurso del futuro.

El Buen Ciudadano reconoce los problemas sociales de los tiempos y tiene la voluntad y capacidad de poder luchar hacia su solución.

El buen ciudadano reconoce y trata de ayudar en la resolución de problemas sociales; problemas de raza, de religión, de economía, problemas políticos en el papel del gobierno con relación al pueblo; problemas de los Estados Unidos en su lugar de los asuntos del mundo; problemas del uso equitativo de los recursos; problemas de familia, de escuela, de la comunidad y el vivir en el vecindario.

El Buen Ciudadano se da cuenta y toma la responsabilidad de llenar las necesidades básicas humanas.

El buen ciudadano se da cuenta de la importancia de resolver las necesidades humanas y se preocupa por la extensión de lo esencial de la vida para más individuos. Toda la gente tiene ciertas necesidades básicas; la necesidad de estar libre de agresiones, dominación, o explotación; la necesidad por el amor y el cariño; la necesidad de pertenecer a grupos y de aceptar ayuda de otros; la necesidad de un nivel de vida que provee una salud adecuada, alojamiento y recreación; la necesidad de tener metas altas de valores espirituales, éticos y morales. El no cumplir las necesidades fundamentales humanas puede resultar en el desarrollo del desajuste lo cual aumenta de la intensidad de los problemas sociales.

El Buen Ciudadano tiene en su posesión y usa su conocimiento, habilidades y destreza en una sociedad democrática.

El buen ciudadano tiene el conocimiento de las capacidades y la destreza a través de su facilidad en la lectura, en el escuchar, en las pláticas y en la observación.

world relationships. He practices the kinds of human relationships that are consistent with a democratic society. He personalizes what happens to others, thereby earning respect and confidence. He develops his own ability to cooperate with others. He sincerely desires to help other persons. Through these practices, he builds good will as a resource for the future.

The Good Citizen recognizes the social problems of the times and has the will and the ability to work toward their solutions.

The good citizen recognizes and endeavors to help in the solution of social problems; problems of race, religion, economics, politics-problems of the role of government in relation to the people; problems of the United States in the place of world affairs; problems of the equitable use of resources; problems of family, school, community, and neighborhood living.

The Good Citizen is aware of and takes responsibility for meeting basic human needs.

The good citizen is aware of the importance of meeting human needs and is concerned with the extension of the essentials of life to more individuals. All people have certain basic human needs; the need to be free from aggression, domination, or exploitation; the need for love and affection; the need to belong to groups and to be helped by others; the need for a level of living which provides for adequate health, housing, and recreation; the need to have high standards of spiritual, ethical, and moral values. The failure to meet these fundamental human needs may result in the development of maladjustments which increase the intensity of social problems.

The Good Citizen possesses and uses knowledge, skills, and abilities necessary in a democratic society.

Usa sus habilidades y capacidades para obtener una
comprensión de la estructura presente y el funcionamiento
de la sociedad, los principios de los trámites de un gobierno
representativo, el impacto de los grupos que ponen
presioness, la operación del sistema económico, la
categorización de la herencia compleja social. Con su base
del conocimiento, de sus capacidades y sus habilidades, el
buen ciudadano se vuelve proficiente en la acción cívica.

(*Estudio de la Educación de Ciudadanía de Detroit)

El Credo Americano
—William Tyler Page

Creo en los Estados Unidos de América como un Gobierno del
pueblo, por el pueblo y para el pueblo; cuyos poderes justos se derivan del
consentimiento de los gobernados; una democracia en una república; una
Nación soberana de muchos estados soberanos; una Unión perfecta, una e
inseparable; establecida sobre los principios de libertad, igualdad, justicia
y humanidad por cual los patriotas Americanos sacrificaron sus vidas y
sus fortunas.

Por eso, creo que es mi deber a mi país el amarlo, apoyar su
Constitución; obedecer sus leyes; respetar su bandera; y defenderlo contra
todos sus enemigos.

Nuestro Himno Nacional

Esta canciónse convirtió en nuestro himno nacional por un decreto
del Congreso el 3 de marzo de 1931. Fue escrito durante la guerra de 1812
por un abogado de Baltimore que había observado el ataque británico a
Fort McHenry. El ataque duró toda la noche y cuando amaneció y se
podía ver 12 bandera de los Estados Unidos ondear sobre el fuerte, él
expresó su orgullo con las siguientes palabras.

The good citizen possesses knowledge, skills, and abilities through facility in reading, listening, discussing, and observing. He uses these skills and abilities in order to gain understanding of the present structure and functioning of society, the working principles of representative government, the impact of pressure groups, the operation of the economic system, the social stratification of the population, and the relationship of all these to the complex social heritage. With knowledge, skills, and abilities as a basis, the good citizen becomes more proficient in civic action.

(*Detroit Citizenship Education Study)

The American's Creed
— William Tyler Page

I BELIEVE in the United States of America as a Government of the people, by the people, for the people; whose just powers are derived from the consent of the governed; a democracy in a republic; a sovereign Nation of many sovereign States; a perfect Union, one and inseparable; established upon those principles of freedom, equality, justice, and humanity for which American patriots sacrificed their lives and fortunes.

I therefore believe it is my duty to my country to love it; to support its Constitution; to obey its laws; to respect its flag; and to defend it against all enemies.

Our National Anthem

This song became our national anthem by an act of Congress on March 3, 1931. It was written during the war of 1812 by a Baltimore lawyer who had watched the British attack on Fort McHenry. The attack lasted all night long, and when dawn came and the United States flag could be seen still flying over the Fort, he expressed his pride with these words.

La Bandera de Estrellas Brillant es
Por Francis Scott Key

Oh qué no puedes ver, a la luz del amanecer,
    Lo que orgullosamente alabamos en el ocaso del crepúscolo?
Cuyas anchas barras y estrellas brillantes en batalla peligrosa,
    Desde los bastiones las vimos galanas ondear?
Y los cohetes refulgentes y las bombas estallando en el aire,
    Dieron prueba durante la noche que nuestra bandera ahí estaba.
Oh la Bandera de Estrellas Brillantes ondea todavía
    Sobrfe la tierra de la gente libre y el hogar de los valientes!

Nuestro Lema Nacional

De acuerdo con la ley Pública Número 851, aprobada en la Segunda sesión del octogésimo-cuarto Congreso de los Estados Unidos, el 30 de julio de 1956, el Lema Nacional de los Estados Unidos es: "EN DIOS CONFIAMOS".

El Gran Sello

En 1792 los Estados Unidos adoptaron el diseño de enseguida como el sello de los Estados Unidos. Un águila calva de alas abiertas con las flechas de la guerra en sus garras y la rama de olivo de la paz representan la guerza y la libertad de la nación. El uso de este sello está estrictamente limitado por ley para autentificar ciertos papeles del gobierno.

The Star-Spangled Banner
by Francis Scott Key

Oh say! can you see, by the dawn's early light,
What so proudly we hailed at the twilight's last gleaming?
Whose broad stripes and bright stars through the perilous fight,
O'er the ramparts we watched were so gallantly streaming?
And the rockets' red glare, the bombs bursting in air,
Gave proof through the night that our flag was still there.
Oh say does the Star-spangled Banner yet wave
O'er the land of the free and the home of the brave!

Our National Motto

In accordance with Public Law Number 851, passed at the Second Session of the 84th Congress of the United States, July 30, 1956, the National Motto of the United States is "IN GOD WE TRUST."

The Great Seal

In 1792 the United States adopted the design below as the seal of the United States. A spread-winged bald eagle brandishing the arrows of war and the olive branch of peace represents the strength and liberty of the nation. Use of this seal is strictly limited by law to authenticate certain government papers.

THE GREAT SEAL OF THE UNITED STATES OF AMERICA

OUR NATIONAL MOTTO "IN GOD WE TRUST"

Los Días Festivos

Técnicamente, no hay días festivos *nccionales* en los Estados Unidos. El Presidente y el Congreso pueden legalmente designar los días festivos únicamente para el Distrito de Columbia y para todos los empleados del gobierno federal. Cada estado tiene el poder de decidir cuáles son sus propios días festivos legales. Sin embargo, la mayoría de los estados observan los días festivos federales legales. Enseguida se enlistan los principales:

Año Nuevo..1° de enero

Día de Martin Luther King, Jr.......................... tercer lunes de enero

Natalicio de Lincoln...12 de febrero

Natalicio de Washington...................................tercer lunes en febrero
    (también conocido como Día del Presidente)

Viernes Santo... viernes anterior a la Pascua
    (observado solamente parte del día en algunos estados)

Día del Recuerdo .... último lunes de mayo

Día de la Independencia................................. 4 de julio

Día del Trabajo... primer lunes de septiembre

Día de Colón... segundo lunes de octubre

Día de los Veteranos... segundo lunes de noviembre

Día de dar Gracias...cuarto jueves de noviembre

Navidad...25 de diciembre

Cuando un día festivo cae en domingo o sábado, es observado usualmente el siguiente lunes o el viernes anterior. En algunos días festivos, las prácticas de cierre del gobierno y los negocios varían.

Holidays

Technically, there are no *national* holidays in the United States. The President and Congress can legally designate holidays only for the District of Columbia and all employees of the federal government. Each state has the power to decide on their own legal holidays. However, most states do observe the federal legal holidays. The major ones are listed below:

New Year's Day .... January 1

Martin Luther King, Jr. Day .... Third Monday in January

Lincoln's Birthday .... February 12

Washington's Birthday .... Third Monday in February
(also called President's Day)

Good Friday.................................... Friday preceding Easter
(observed for only part of the day in some states)

Memorial Day .... Last Monday in May

Independence Day.......................... July 4

Labor Day .... First Monday in September

Columbus Day .... Second Monday in October

Veterans' Day................................. Second Monday in November

Thanksgiving Day .... Fourth Thursday in November

Christmas .... December 25

When a holiday falls on a Sunday or a Saturday, it is usually observed on the following Monday or the Friday before. For some holidays, government and business closing practices vary.

Apéndice 1

Las excepciones para residencia y los requisitos de presencia fisica

Excepciones para el casado(a) aon ciudadano(a):

Una excepción al requisito de 5 años de residencia se hace en el caso de tener esposo(a) ciudadano(a), y puede ser usted elegible a solicitar la ciudadanía después de sólo 3 años. Para hacerse elegible, el extranjero debe de haber estado casado y viviendo con ciudadano de los Estados Unidos por tres años, y el esposo o la esposa debe haber sido ciudadano por los tres años completos. Un solicitante debe de haber estado físicamente presente en los Estados Unidos al menos 50% del período de tiempo (o 18 meses) para calificar para la ciudadanía.

Residencia de los ultimos seis meses:

Inmediatatemente antes de registrar su petición, el solicitante debe de haber sido residente del estado o distrito del INS adonde está registrando su petición.

Viajes afuera y el requisito de residencia:

El solicitante no está obligado a quedarse en los Estados Unidos durante cada día del periódo de los 5 años. Puede usted hacer visitas cortas afuera de los Estados Unidos sea antes o despues de solicitar la naturalización y puede incluir como parte del requerimiento de la residencia de 5 años, el tiempo que estuvo ausente. Sin embargo, hay límites estrictos para la cantidad de tiempo que se le permite estar afuera:
1. No debe de estar ausente de los Estados Unidos por un período constante de un año o más y,
2. No debe usted estar fuera de los Estados Unidos por un total combinado de más de 30 meses durante los ultimos 5 años.

Appendix 1

Exceptions to Residence and Physical Presence Requirements

Exceptions for a citizen spouse:

An exception to the 5 year residency requirement is made in the case of the spouse of a United States citizen, who **may** be eligible to apply for citizenship after only 3 years. In order to be eligible, the alien must have been married to and living with the United States citizen for three years, and the spouse must have been a United States citizen for the entire three years. An applicant must have been physically present in the United States for at least 50% of the time period (or 18 months) in order to qualify to apply for citizenship.

Residency for the last three months:

Immediately prior to filing the petition, the applicant must have been a resident of the state or INS District where the petition is being filed.

Trips away and the residency requirement:

The applicant is not obliged to stay in the United States during every day of the 5 year period. You can make short visits outside the United States either before or after applying for naturalization, and may include as part of the required 5 years' residence the time you were absent. However, there are strict limitations on the amount of time you can be away:
1. You must not be absent from the United States for a continuous period of one year or more and;
2. You must not be out of the United States for a combined total of more than 30 months during the last 5 years.

Si está ausente por un año o más en cualquier tiempo durante el período de 5 años antes de iniciar la petición, esto interrumpe su período de residencia para la naturalización. Esto es verdad aunque haya obtenido un permiso de volver a entrar del Servicio de Inmigración y Naturalización. Cuando se interrumpe el periodo de residencia, se tiene que completar después de regresar usted a los Estados Unidos. Esto quiere decir que tendrá que esperar al menos 4 años y un día despues de regresar antes de iniciar su solicitud. Además, si durante el período de los 5 años, usted ha estado ausente por un total de más de 30 meses, entonces tendrá que quedarse en los Estados Unidos hasta que haya permanecido al menos 30 meses de los ultimos 5 años antes de llenar la petición para naturalización en la corte.

Casos especiales que le disculpan su ausencia de más de un año

En ciertos casos especiales, usted puede conservar su residencia que haya acumulado por motivo de la naturalización, aunque se quede afuera de los Estados Unidos por más tiempo que un año. En estos casos especiales, el tiempo que pasa usted en el extranjero se puede contar como parte de su período de residencia. Esta excepción a las reglas generales de residencia es para la gente trabajando en ciertos sectores específicos privados y públicos, y para las organizaciones religiosas.

Para obtener permiso de conservar su residencia, tiene usted que iniciar la solicitud N-470 (véase el ejemplar), **antes** de salir de los Estados Unidos. En la mayoría de los casos, las personas que buscan conservar su residencia tienen que ser residentes permanentes legales que han vivido en los Estados Unidos por un período sin interrupción de al menos un año, con ninguna ausencia de cualquier clase. Los reglamentos son diferentes para los trabajadores religiosos que salen afuera para desempeñar sus deberes religiosos; ellos pueden hacer solicitud al regresar a los Estados Unidos.

Presentar un N-470 no le disculpa al extranjero de su requisito de obtener un permiso para volver a entrar antes de cualquier viaje afuera del país de un año o más largo. No le alivia al solicitante de los 30 meses del requisito de presencia física (véase arriba).

If you are absent for one year or more at any time during the 5-year period just before filing the petition, this breaks the naturalization residence period. This is true even if you obtained a re-entry permit from the Immigration and Naturalization Service. When the residence period is broken, a new period of residence will have to be completed after returning to the United States. This means that you will have to wait at least 4 years and one day after coming back before filing your application. Furthermore, if during the 5-year period you have been absent for a total of more than 30 months, you will have to stay in the United States until you have been physically present for at least 30 months out of the last 5 years before filing the petition for naturalization in court.

Special cases excusing absences over one year:

In certain special cases, you may be able to preserve residency previously accumulated for naturalization purposes, even when you stay outside the United States for longer than one year. In these special cases, the time spent abroad may be counted as part of the residence period. This exception to the general residence rules is for people working in certain specified U.S. private and public sectors, and religious organizations.

To obtain permission to preserve residency, you have to file an N-470 application (see sample) **before** departing from the United States. In most cases, persons seeking to preserve their residency must be lawful permanent residents who have lived in the United States for an uninterrupted period of at least one year, without any absences whatsoever. The regulations are different for religious workers going abroad to perform religious duties — they can apply after they return to the United States.

Filing an N-470 does not excuse the alien from the requirement of obtaining a re-entry permit in advance of any trips out of the country of a year or longer. It does not relieve the applicant from the 30 months physical presence requirement (see above).

Miembros extranjeros de las Fuerzas Armadas Del E.U. y esposos de ciudadanos empleados en el extranjero

Las excepciones al requisito de residencia tocante a las ausencias de un año también se hacen para los miembros extranjeros de las fuerzas armadas de los Estados Unidos, y por los esposos de ciudadanos empleados en el extranjero por ciertas organizaciones de E.U. que tienen que acompañar a sus esposos ciudadanos en conexión con tal empleo. Un empleado del gobierno de los Estados Unidos en el extranjero que ha presentado el Formulario N-470, se le considera estar físicamente presente en los Estados Unidos durante se empleo en el extranjero. Un Formulario N-426 (véase el ejemplar) se usa por las personas que estan en el servicio o han prestado servicio honorable en las fuerzas armadas de los Estados Unidos incluyendo sus componentes de la reserva.

Alien members of the U.S. Armed Forces, and spouses of certain citizens employed abroad:

Exceptions to the residency requirement regarding absences for more than one year are also made for alien members of the United States armed forces, and for spouses of citizens employed abroad by certain U.S. organizations who must accompany their citizen spouses in connection with such employment. An employee of the United States government abroad, who has filed Form N-470, is considered as being physically present in the United States during such employment abroad. A Form N-426 (see sample) is used by persons who are serving or have served honorably under specific conditions in the United States armed forces, including the reserve components.

Form N-470
Application to Preserve Residence

UNITED STATES DEPARTMENT OF JUSTICE
Immigration and Naturalization Service

OMB No. 1115-0014

APPLICATION TO PRESERVE RESIDENCE
FOR NATURALIZATION PURPOSES

(Under Section 316(b) or 317, Immigration and Nationality Act)

(Please read instructions)

Take or mail to:
Immigration and Naturalization Service

Fee Stamp

Alien Registration No.

Date of Birth   Place of Birth

1. My full true name is ....

2. My home address in the United States is ....
   (Number and street)

   ....
   (City or town)   (State)   (Zip code)

   My foreign address (☐ is ☐ will be) ....
   (Number and street)

   ....
   (City or town)   (State)

3. I am an alien. I was lawfully admitted to the United States for permanent residence at ....

   .... under the name of ....
   (Port of entry)

   on .... on the vessel ....
   (Month) (Day) (Year)   (if otherwise than vessel show manner of arrival)

   I have resided in and have been physically present in the United States for an uninterrupted period of at least .... year(s) since such lawful entry. Since the date of my lawful entry, I have been absent from the United States as follows (include date of last departure if now abroad, and if necessary attach an additional sheet to show all absences):

Date of departure	Date and port of return	Name of vessel	Purpose of trip

4. Since becoming a permanent resident, have you ever filed an income tax return as a nonresident alien or otherwise claimed or received benefits as a nonresident alien under the income tax laws? ☐ Yes ☐ No

5. I (☐ am, ☐ will be, ☐ was) employed as, or under contract as, ...

   by ....
   (Name of employer)

   address ....
   (Number and street)   (City or town)   (State)   (Zip code)

   Such employment of contract { necessitates / will necessitate / necessitated } my presence in ....
   (Country or countries)

   from .... to ....
   (Month) (Day) (Year)   (Month) (Day) (Year)

6. My absence from the United States for such periods (☐ is, ☐ will be, ☐ was):
   - ☐ on behalf of the United States Government.
   - ☐ for the purpose of carrying on scientific research on behalf of an American institution of research.
   - ☐ for the purpose of engaging in the development of foreign trade and commerce of the United States on behalf of an American firm or corporation or a subsidiary thereof engaged in the development of such trade and commerce.
   - ☐ necessary to the protection of the property rights abroad of an American firm or corporation engaged in the development of foreign trade and commerce of the United States.
   - ☐ on behalf of a public international organization of which the United States is a member, by which I was first employed on .... , 19..........
   - ☐ solely in my capacity as a ☐ clergyman, ☐ missionary, ☐ brother, ☐ nun, or ☐ sister.

7. In support of the foregoing statement of facts I submit the following documents ....

   ....
   (See instructions)

8. I respectfully request that you find my absence under the above-stated conditions to be in compliance with the provisions of Sec. 316(b) or 317 of the Immigration and Nationality Act.

9. The following lawful permanent resident members of my immediate family [spouse and or child(ren) only] will be residing abroad as dependent members of my household, whom I also desire to receive the benefits hereunder:

Name	"A" Number	Relationship	Marital Status

Signature of Person Preparing Form, If Other Than Applicant	Signature of Applicant
I declare that this document was prepared by me at the request of the applicant and is based on all information of which I have any knowledge.	I certify that the above statements are true and correct to the best of my knowledge and belief.
SIGNATURE	COMPLETE SIGNATURE OF APPLICANT
ADDRESS DATE	MAILING ADDRESS Number, Street, City, State, and ZIP Code DATE

Form N-470 (Rev. 10-1-85)Y

Form N-426
Certification of Military Service

Form Approved
OMB No. 43-R0265

UNITED STATES DEPARTMENT OF JUSTICE IMMIGRATION AND NATURALIZATION SERVICE **REQUEST FOR** **CERTIFICATION OF MILITARY OR NAVAL SERVICE** (SUBMIT IN TRIPLICATE)	ALIEN REGISTRATION NO. _____	DATE OF REQUEST

For use in connection with my petition for naturalization, please complete the certification of military service on the reverse and furnish it to the office of the Immigration and Naturalization Service shown in the address block below. The information shown below is furnished to help locate and identify my military records. APPLICANT: FURNISH AS MUCH INFORMATION AS POSSIBLE. IF YOU WERE ISSUED A REPORT OF SEPARATION, DD FORM 214, ATTACH A COPY. FILL IN THE BLANKS ON THIS PAGE ONLY. PLEASE TYPE OR PRINT CLEARLY. PRESS FIRMLY–ALL COPIES MUST BE LEGIBLE. (DO NOT USE PENCIL)

NAME USED DURING ACTIVE SERVICE (Last, first, middle)	SOCIAL SECURITY NO.	DATE OF BIRTH	PLACE OF BIRTH

For an effective records search, it is important that ALL periods of service be shown below. (Use blank sheet if more space is needed.)

ACTIVE SERVICE:

BRANCH OF SERVICE (Show also last organization if known.)	DATE ENTERED ON ACTIVE DUTY	DATE RELEASED FROM ACTIVE DUTY	CHECK WHICH OFFICER	ENLISTED	SERVICE NUMBER DURING THIS PERIOD

RESERVE OR NATIONAL GUARD SERVICE: ⟶ If none, check ☐ None

BRANCH OF SERVICE	CHECK WHICH RESERVE	N GUARD	DATE MEMBERSHIP BEGAN	DATE MEMBERSHIP ENDED	CHECK WHICH OFFICER	ENLISTED	SERVICE NUMBER DURING THIS PERIOD

ARE YOU A MILITARY RETIREE OR FLEET RESERVIST? ☐ No ☐ Yes

SIGNATURE (Present Name)	PRESENT ADDRESS (Number, Street, City, State, and ZIP Code)

INSTRUCTIONS TO CERTIFYING OFFICER

Persons who are serving or have served honorably under specified conditions in the armed forces of the United States, inclusive of the reserve components of the armed forces of the United States, are granted certain exemptions from the general requirements for naturalization. The law requires such service to be established by a duly authenticated copy of the records of the executive department having custody of the record of service, showing whether the serviceman served honorably in an active-duty status, a reserve-duty status, or both, and whether each separation from the service was under honorable conditions. For that purpose, the certified statement on the reverse of this form, executed under the seal of your department, is required and should cover not only the period(s) of service shown above, but any other periods of service (active, reserve, or both) rendered by the serviceman.

The reverse of this form should be completed, or the information called for furnished by separate letter, and the form and letter returned to the office of the Immigration and Naturalization Service at the address in the box immediately below.

Immigration and Naturalization Service

 RETURN TO

Please type or print complete return address. Include ZIP code.

Form N–426 (Rev.5–12–77)N

Apéndice 2

La Provision "Rollback" y los Requisitos de Residencia

Para calificar para la naturalización, los residentes permanentes legales comienzan a contar su tiempo de 5 años que necesitan tener en los Estados Unidos desde el tiempo que sean oficialmente admitidos en este país como residentes permanentes. Hay excepciones a esta regla, sin embargo, que les permite a ciertos grupos de refugiados poder comenzar a acumular la residencia de los 5 años necesitados antes de que sean admitidos oficialmente como residentes permanentes.

La Ley de los Refugiados Cubanos de 1966, la ley de los Indochinos de 1977, y ciertos refugiados cubiertos por la Ley Pública 95-412, adoptada en 1978, incluyen lo que se llama la provisión del "rollback". Esta provisión le permite al Servicio de Inmigración y Naturalización considerar a un refugiado como legalmente admitido para residencia permanente en alguna fecha antes que la fecha cuando el refugiado recibe su residencia permanente en la realidad. Así es que un refugiado Cubano o Indochino que se hace residente permanente y más tarde busca solicitar su naturalización, recibe crédito por el tiempo que pasó aquí como refugiado. Normalmente, el "rollback" se aplica en el tiempo que el refugiado cambia su estado a residente permanente. Sin embargo la ley también hace provisión de mover hacia atrás la fecha de ciertos otros refugiados, aún después que se han hecho residentes permanentes legales.

Los grupos individuales de refugiados son examinados con más detalle abajo. Si después de leer este material aquí abajo, que tenga que ver con su propia situación, usted tiene alguna pregunta, puede recibir ayuda al llamar a la oficina del INS que le queda más cerca (véase Apéndice 4).

Appendix 2

The Rollback Provision and Residency Requirements

To qualify for naturalization, most lawful permanent residents begin counting their required 5 years residence in the United States from the time they are admitted officially to this country as permanent residents. There are exceptions to this rule, however, which permit certain refugee groups to begin accumulating the required 5-year residence before they actually become officially admitted as permanent residents.

The Cuban Refugee Act of 1966, the Indochinese Act of 1977, and certain refugees covered by Public Law 95-412, adopted in 1978, include what is called a "rollback" provision. This provision allows the Immigration and Naturalization Service to consider a refugee as having been lawfully admitted for permanent residence at some date earlier than the date the refugee was actually granted permanent residence. Thus, a Cuban or Indochinese refugee who becomes a permanent resident and later seeks to apply for naturalization is given credit for the time spent here as a refugee. Normally, the "rollback" is applied at the time the refugee changes status to permanent resident. However, the law also makes provision to roll back the date on certain other refugees, even after they have become lawful permanent residents.

Individual refugee groups are examined in more detail below. If, after reading the material below which concerns your own situation you have any questions, you can get help by calling your nearest INS office (see Appendix 4).

Los efugiados Indochinos:

La Ley Pública 95-145 provee el mover hacia atrás la fecha de admisión del refugiado a residencia permanente legal hasta lo que sea más reciente:
1. 31 de marzo de 1975, o
2. la fecha actual de admisión o libertad condicional, o
3. la fecha actual de admisión del padre o esposo como residente permanente legal, si el solicitante es un esposo no refugiado, o menor de edad soltero, o una persona que se ajustó como refugiado.

Como se indicó aquí arriba, es importante que usted comprenda que al aplicar la provisión del rollback, que use la fecha mas reciente de las nombradas arriba que en realidad se puede aplicar a su caso. Por ejemplo, si un refugiado Indochino entró a un campamento de reestablecimiento en los Estados Unidos el 10 de marzo de 1975, pero no fué inspeccionado y admitido o puesto en libertad condicional oficialmente por el Servicio de Inmigración y Naturalización hasta el 5 de agosto de 1975, el rollback no comenzaría hasta la fecha más reciente, y naturalmente eso sería el 5 de agosto de 1975. Otro ejemplo, si un refugiado Indochino fue ajustado como residente permanente legal entre el 31 de marzo de 1975 y el 28 de octubre de 1977 a través de los procedimientos regulares de inmigración y ajuste, esa persona puede solicitar los beneficios del "rollback". La solicitud se hace en el mismo formulario usado para los ajustes regulares del refugiado Indochino, y debe de ser completado antes de que el solicitante inicie su naturalización.

Los refugiados Cubanos:

La Ley de Refugiados Cubanos de 1966 provee un "rollback" de la fecha de admisión del refugiado como residente permanente a la más reciente de las fechas que siguen:
1. la fecha actual de admisión o libertad condicional a los Estados Unidos, o
2. treinta meses antes de iniciar una solicitud para ajuste a residencia permanente, o
3. el 2 de mayo de 1964.

Indochinese refugees:

Public Law 95-145 provides for the rollback of a refugee's date of admission for lawful permanent residence to whichever of the following comes latest:
1. March 31, 1975, or
2. The actual date of admission or parole, or
3. Date of parent or spouse's admission for lawful permanent residence, if the applicant is a non-refugee spouse, or minor unmarried child, or a person adjusted as a refugee.

As indicated above, it is important for you to understand that in applying the rollback provision, you use the **latest** of the above dates which actually applies in your case. For example, if an Indochinese refugee entered a resettlement camp in the United States on March 10, 1975, but was not inspected and admitted or paroled officially by the Immigration and Naturalization Service until August 5, 1975, the rollback would begin on the later date, which of course would be August 5, 1975. In another example, if an Indochinese refugee was adjusted to lawful permanent residence between March 31, 1975 and October 28, 1977 through the regular immigration and adjustment procedures, that person can apply for the rollback benefits. Application is made on the same form used for the regular Indochinese refugee adjustments, and should be completed before the applicant files for naturalization.

Cuban refugees:

The Cuban Refugee Act of 1966 provides for the rollback of a refugee's date of admission for lawful permanent residence to the latest of the following dates:
1. Actual date of admission or parole into the United States, or
2. Thirty months before filing an application for adjustment to permanent resident, or
3. May 2, 1964.

La Ley Pública 95-412:

Bajo la L.P. 95-412, ciertos refugiados con libertad condicional en los Estados Unidos antes del primero de abril de 1980 que adquirieron su estado civil como residente permanente legal bajo alguna otra provisión de la ley, pueden hacer que su fecha se mueva hacia atrás hasta la fecha de su libertad condicional original dentro del país.

La Ley Pública 96-212:

Este es La Ley de los Refugiados de 1980, la cual amplifica la definición básica del "refugiado" y aumenta su admisión a los Estados Unidos anualmente. También contiene una provisión de "rollback" que beneficia a las personas que han sido admitidas como refugiadas, o quienes después de su entrada se les ha otorgado estado civil como refugiados. Estas personas no son elegibles para solicitar su estado civil de residente permanente hasta que hayan estado presentes físicamente en los Estados Unidos por un año después de su entrada como refugiado o un año después de ser clasificados como refugiados. Sin embargo, esta provisión del "rollback" que les permite a tales personas tener su fecha de residencia permanente legal registrada desde la fecha de su entrada como refugiado, (o en el caso de personas clasificadas como refugiados después de su entrada a los Estados Unidos) movida hacia atrás un año antes de la aprobación de su solicitud para la residencia permanente. Ciertos refugiados admitidos a los Estados Unidos antes del 1 de abril de 1980, pueden ser elegibles para las provisiones del "rollback" y deben consultar con su oficina del Servicio de Inmigración y Naturalización para aclarar sus propios casos.

Public Law 95-412:

Under P.L. 95-412, certain refugees paroled into the United States before April 1, 1980, who acquired the status of lawful permanent resident under some other provision of the law, may have their date of permanent residence rolled back to the date of their original parole into the country.

Public Law 96-212:

This is the Refugee Act of 1980, which broadens the basic definition of "refugee" and increases their admission into the United States on an annual basis. It also contains a rollback provision benefiting persons who have been admitted as refugees, or who after entry have been granted status as refugees. These persons are not eligible to apply for permanent resident status until they have been physically present in the United States for one year after entry as a refugee, or one year after being classified as a refugee. However, there is a rollback provision which allows such persons to have their date of lawful permanent residence recorded as of the date of their entry as a refugee, or in the case of persons classified as refugees after entry into the United States, rolled back one year before approval of their application for permanent residence. Certain refugees admitted to the United States before April 1, 1980 may be eligible for other rollback provisions and should consult their local Immigration and Naturalization Service office for clarification of their cases.

Apéndice 3

Reputación y Lealdad

Como solicitante para la ciudadanía de E.U., usted debe de mostrar haber sido una persona de buena reputación durante todos sus 5 años antes de iniciar su petición de naturalización, y hasta que el juez decida si califica para naturalizarse.

La ley declara que no puede considerarse que tiene una reputación buena si es que viene usted de alguna de las siguientes clases en cualquier tiempo durante su período de 5 años y hasta que esté verdaderamente naturalizado:

1. borracho consuetudinario
2. polígamo, adultero, personas conectadas con la prostitución o narcóticos, criminales;
3. los jugadores convictos, personas que reciben su ingreso principal del juego ilegal;
4. personas convictas y encarceladas por 180 días o más;
5. personas que mienten bajo juramento para obtener algún beneficio bajo las leyes de inmigración y naturalización;
6. personas convictas de homicidio en cualquier tiempo.

Las descalificaciones en lista aquí arriba no son las únicas razones por las cuales se puede determinar que una persona una buena reputación. Otras clases de conducta se pueden tomar en consideración por el juez al decidir si un solicitante tiene una buena reputación requerida para volverse ciudadano. Por ejemplo, el juez tiene derecho a considerar las acciones de abuso de criaturas o de esposas, asaltos físicos, obscenidad, el registro de bancarrota o el no hacer sus pagos de manutención de hijos tal como fue ordenado en un divorcio — cualesquier acciones que sean contrarias a las costumbres y normas de la comunidad.

A los extranjeros que no hayan desempeñado sus deberes de servicio en las fuerzas armadas de los Estados Unidos durante un tiempo

Appendix 3

Character and Loyalty

As an applicant for U. S. citizenship, you must show that you have been a person of good moral character during all of the 5 years before filing the petition for naturalization, and until the judge decides that you qualify for naturalization.

The law states that you cannot be considered to be of good moral character if you come within any of the following classes at any time during the 5-year period and up until you are actually naturalized:

1. Habitual drunkards;
2. Polygamists, adulterers, persons connected with prostitution or narcotics, criminals;
3. Convicted gamblers, persons getting their principal income from illegal gambling;
4. Persons convicted and jailed for 180 days or more;
5. Persons who lie under oath to gain a benefit under the immigration and naturalization laws;
6. Persons convicted of murder at any time.

The disqualifications listed above are not the only reasons for which a person may be found to lack good moral character. Other types of behavior may be taken into consideration by the judge in deciding whether an applicant has the good moral character required to become a citizen. For example, the judge would be entitled to consider acts of child or spouse abuse, physical assaults, obscenity, filing bankruptcy, or failing to pay child support payments ordered by a court — any acts which are contrary to mores and standards of the community.

Aliens who have not performed their duties to serve in the armed forces of the United States during a time of war may be denied

de guerra se les puede prohibir la ciudadanía. Esto incluye las personas que hayan sido convictas de haber dejado sin permiso su servicio o de haber esquivado el servicio como a las personas que hayan solicitado y hayan recibido exenciones al servicio basándose en el hecho de ser extranjeros.

Es de suma importancia que la pregunta sobre la solicitud tocante al arresto se conteste completamente y correctamente. El no revelar un arresto puede resultar en que le nieguen su petición de naturalización o le revoquen a una persona su naturalización. Todos los arrestos se deben de revelar, a pesar de que el arresto no resulte en una convicción. Por ejemplo, si más adelante el arresto fue borrado de su expediente, o si el arresto ocurrió mientras que el solicitante fuese menor, o si el arresto ocurrió en otro país o más de cinco años antes de iniciar la petición, o si el arresto fue una violación de un reglamento del tránsito. Los peticionantes pueden desear entregar copias certificadas de la orden judicial de los arrestos junto con sus solicitudes para la naturalización.

citizenship. These include persons who have been convicted of deserting or evading service as well as persons who applied for and were given exemptions from service on the ground that they were aliens.

It is of extreme importance that the question on the application concerning arrest be answered completely and accurately. Failure to reveal an arrest could result in denial of the petition for naturalization or revocation of a person's naturalization. All arrests should be revealed, even if the arrest does not result in conviction. For example, if the arrest was later expunged from the record, or if the arrest occurred while the applicant was a juvenile, or if the arrest occurred in another country or more than five years before filing of the petition, or if the arrest was only a violation of a traffic regulation. Petitioners may wish to submit certified copies of the court's disposition of their arrest(s) with their applications for naturalization.

Appendix 4
INS Offices in the U.S.A.

The District Offices are listed first, followed by a list of other INS offices. Both lists are arranged in zip code order so you can find the city nearest you. When sending mail to these offices, be sure to put "U. S. Immigration Service" at the top of the address.

District Offices

G.P.O. Box 5068
Federal Building (Hato Rey)
San Juan, PR 00936
(809) 766-5329

Federal Bldg., Room E-123
Government Center
Boston, MA 02203
(617) 565-3879

739 Warren Avenue
Portland, ME 04103
(207) 780-3352

Federal Building
970 Broad Street
Newark, NJ 07102
(201) 645-4400

26 Federal Plaza
New York, NY 10278
(212) 206-6500

68 Court Street
Buffalo, NY 14202
(716) 849-6760

U.S. Courthouse, Room 1321
601 Market Street
Philadelphia, PA 19106
(215) 596-1968

E. A. Garmatz Federal Bldg.
101 W. Lombard Street
Baltimore, MD 21201
(301) 962-2065

4420 N. Fairfax Dr. Room 210
Arlington, VA 22203
(202) 307-1501

Federal Bldg., First Floor
77 Forsyth Street S.W.
Atlanta, GA 30303
(404) 331-5158

7880 Biscayne Blvd.
Miami, FL 33130
(305) 536-5741

Federal Bldg., Room 1917
1240 East 9th Street
Cleveland, OH 44199
(216) 522-4770

Federal Building
333 Mt. Elliot Street
Detroit, MI 48207
(313) 226-3290

2901 Metro Drive
Bloomington, MN 55425
(612) 854-7754

Federal Building
301 S. Park, Room 512
Helena, MT 59626
(406) 449-5288

Dirksen Federal Office Bldg.
219 S. Dearborn Street
Chicago, IL 60604
(312) 353-7334

9747 N. Conant Avenue
Kansas City, MO 64153
(816) 891-0603

3736 So. 132nd Street
Omaha, NE 68144
(402) 697-9155

Postal Service Building
701 Loyola Ave., Room 8011
New Orleans, LA 70113
(504) 589-6533

8101 N. Stemmons Fwy.
Dallas, TX 75247
(214) 655-5384

509 North Belt
Main Floor
Houston, TX 77060
(713) 847-7900

U.S. Federal Building
727 E. Durango, #A301
San Antonio, TX 78206
(512) 229-6350

2102 Teege Road
Harlingen, TX 78550
(512) 425-7333

700 E.San Antonio Street
El Paso, TX 79984
(915) 534-6366

4730 Paris Street
Denver, CO 80239
(303) 371-3041

2035 North Central Ave.
Phoenix, AZ 85004
(602) 379-3122

300 N.Los Angeles Street
Los Angeles, CA 90012
(213) 894-2119

880 Front Street
San Diego, CA 92188
(619) 557-5570

Appraisers Building
630 Sansome Street
San Francisco, CA 94111
(415) 705-4411

595 Ala Moana Blvd.
Honolulu, HI 96813
(808) 541-1379

Federal Office Building
511 N.W. Broadway
Portland, OR 97209
(503) 326-3006

815 Airport Way, South
Seattle, WA 98134
(206) 553-5956

620 E. 10th Avenue, #102
Anchorage, AK 99501
(907) 343-7820

INS Sub-Offices which Can Help with Information and Forms

Federal Building, Room 117
Charlotte Amalie
St. Thomas, VI 00801
(809) 774-1390

Federal Building
203 John O. Pastore
Providence, RI 02903
(401) 454-7440

Federal Building
St. Albans, VT 05478
(802) 951-6658

Ribicoff Federal Building
450 Main Street
Hartford, CT 06103
(203) 240-3171

U. S. Post Office
445 Broadway, Room 220
Albany, NY 12207
(518) 472-4621

2130 Federal Building
1000 Liberty Avenue
Pittsburgh, PA 15222
(412) 644-3356

Norfolk Federal Building
200 Granby Mall, Room 439
Norfolk, VA 23510
(804) 441-3081

6 Woodlawn Green, #138
Charlotte, NC 28217
(704) 523-1704

Federal Building, #G-18
400 West Bay Street
Jacksonville, FL 32202
(904) 791-2624

5509 W. Gray Street, #113
Tampa, FL 33609
(813) 228-2131

814 Federal Building
167 N. Main Street
Memphis, TN 38103
(901) 544-3301

U.S. Courthouse, Room 601
West 6th & Broadway
Louisville, KY 40202
(502) 582-6375

Federal Building, #8525
550 North Main Street
Cincinnati, OH 45202
(513) 287-6080

U.S. Federal Building
46 East Ohio Street
Indianapolis, IN 46204
(317) 226-6009

Federal Building, #186
517 E. Wisconsin Avenue
Milwaukee, WI 53202
(414) 297-3565

1222 Spruce Street
Suite 100, First Floor
St. Louis, MO 63103
(314) 539-2532

4149 Highline Blvd., #300
Oklahoma City, OK 73108
(405) 942-8670

230 W. 400 South Street
Salt Lake City, UT 84138
(801) 524-5771

Federal Building, #1114
517 Gold Ave., S.W.
Albuquerque, NM 87103
(505) 766-2378

Federal Building
U.S. Courthouse
300 Las Vegas Blvd. So.
Las Vegas, NV 89101
(702) 384-3696

712 Mill Street, Suite 150
Reno, NV 89502
(702) 784-5427

Federal Building
U.S. Courthouse
1130 "O" Street
Fresno, CA 93721
(209) 487-5091

280 So. First Street
San Jose, CA 95113
(408) 291-7876

711 J Street
Sacramento, CA 95814
(916) 551-2785

Pacific News Building
238 O'Hara Street
Agana, GU 96910
011 (671) 472-7349

691 U.S. Courthouse Bldg.
Spokane, WA 99201
(509) 353-2758

Appendix 5
INS Offices Outside the U.S.A.

Note: Some of the addresses below contain an "APO" which stands for "Army or Airforce Post Office." This means that your letter will go by U.S. mail to the APO in the United States, and from there it will be handled by the military to its foreign destination. Mail sent to a Fleet Post Office (FPO) is similarly handled by the Navy. Postage rates are the same as for any mail inside the U.S., and is carried at no extra charge to the final destination.

American Embassy
91 Vasilissis Sophias
Athens, Greece
APO New York 09253
71-2951

American Embassy
Bangkok Thailand
APO San Francisco 96346
252-5040, Ext. 2614 or 2615

American Consulate General
Siesmayerstrasse 21
6 Frankfurt/Main Germany
Box 12, APO New York 09757
74 00 71

American Consulate, Box 30
Room 39 St. John's Bldg.
Garden Road, Hong Kong
FPO, San Francisco 96659
23-9011, Ext 262 or 337

American Embassy
1201 Roxas Building
Manila, Phillippines
APO San Francisco 96528
59-80-11, Ext. 694 or 695

American Embassy
Paseo de la Reforma 305
Mexico 5, D.F.
(905) 553-3333, Ext. 492

American Consulate General
41 Ave. Constitucion Poniente
Monterrey, N.L., Mexico
43-06-50, Ext 27 and 68

American Consulate General
Piazza della Republica
Naples, Italy
Box 18 FPO New York 09521
660-966

American Embassy
Via V. Veneto 119
Rome, Italy
APO New York 09794
4674

American Embassy
Seoul, Korea
APO San Francisco 96301

American Embassy
2 Friedrich Schmidt Platz
1010 **Vienna, Austria**
346611, Ext 2355

Appendix 6
Information Concerning Citizenship Education to Meet Naturalization Requirements

Immigration and Naturalization Service
Information Bulletin Re: Naturalizations Requirements

A person who is applying for naturalization as a citizen of the United States generally is required to show that he has some knowledge and understanding of the English language and of the history and form of government of the United States. Certain persons are exempted from the English requirements and may become citizens even though they cannot read, write or speak English. The exact requirements, and the exemptions from them, are stated below:

1. The applicant has to be able to speak, read and write simple words in everyday use in the English language.
   Exceptions: A person who is physically unable to speak, read or write English is exempt. The same exemption is given to a person who is either A) over 50 years old and has been living in the United States for periods totaling at least 20 years following lawful admission for permanent residence, or B) over 55 years old and has been living in the United States for periods totaling at least 15 years following lawful admission for permanent residence.
2. The applicant has to be able to sign his name in English.
   Exceptions: An exception is given to any person who qualifies under "A" or "B" in Item #1 above. That person would be permitted to sign his or her name in a foreign language.
3. The applicant has to be familiar with the Constitution and the more important historical facts in the development of the United States, and with the form and principles of our government. There are no exceptions to this requirement. All applicants have to show that they have this knowledge, and they may show this in a foreign language if they are exempt from speaking, reading and writing English according to item #1 above.

The test to determine whether the applicant has the required knowledge of English, history and government is given by a naturalization examiner when the applicant appears before him to file his petition. The test is given orally. The questions asked are in simple English and cover only subjects with which anyone who has made a reasonable effort to learn should be familiar.

Appendix 7

The Constitution of the United States of America

Preamble

WE THE PEOPLE of the United States, in order to form a more perfect Union, establish justice, insure domestic tranquillity, provide for the common defense, promote the general welfare, and secure the blessings of liberty to ourselves and our posterity, do ordain and establish this Constitution for the United States of America.

Article I

Section 1. All legislative powers herein granted shall be vested in a Congress of the United States, which shall consist of a Senate and House of Representatives.

Section 2. The House of Representatives shall be composed of members chosen every second year by the people of the several states, and the electors in each state shall have the qualifications requisite for electors of the most numerous branch of the state legislature.

No person shall be a Representative who shall not have attained to the age of twenty-five years, and been seven years a citizen of the United States, and who shall not, when elected, be an inhabitant of that state in which he shall be chosen.

Representatives and direct taxes shall be apportioned among the several states which may be included within this Union, according to their respective numbers, which shall be determined by adding to the whole number of free persons, including those bound to service for a term of years, and excluding Indians not taxed, three-fifths of all other persons. The actual enumeration shall be made within three years after the first meeting of the Congress of the United States, and within every subsequent term of ten years, in such manner as they shall by law direct. The number of Representatives shall not exceed one for every thirty thousand, but each state shall have at least one representative; and until such enumeration shall be made, the state of New Hampshire shall be entitled to choose three, Massachusetts eight, Rhode Island and Providence Plantations one, Connecticut five, New York six, New Jersey four, Pennsylvania eight, Delaware one, Maryland six, Virginia ten, North Carolina five, South Carolina five, and Georgia three.

When vacancies happen in the representation from any state, the executive authority thereof shall issue writs of election to fill such vacancies.

The House of Representatives shall choose their Speaker and other officers; and shall have the sole power of impeachment.

Section 3. The Senate of the United States shall be composed of two Senators from each state, chosen by the legislature thereof, for six years and each Senator shall have one vote.

Immediately after they shall be assembled in consequence of the first election, they shall be divided as equally as may be into three classes. The seats of the Senators of the first class shall be vacated at the expiration of the second year, of the second class at the expiration of the fourth year, and of the third class at the expiration of the sixth year, so that one-third may be chosen every second year; and if vacancies happen by resignation, or otherwise, during the recess of the legislature of any state, the executive thereof may make temporary appointments until the next meeting of the legislature, which shall then fill such vacancies.

No person shall be a Senator who shall not have attained to the age of thirty years, and been nine years a citizen of the United States, and who shall not, when elected, be an inhabitant of that state for which he shall be chosen.

The Vice President of the United States shall be President of the Senate, but shall have no vote, unless they be equally divided.

The Senate shall choose their other officers, and also a President pro tempore, in the absence of the

Vice President, or when he shall exercise the office of President of the United States.

The Senate shall have the sole power to try all impeachments. When sitting for that purpose, they shall be on oath or affirmation. When the President of the United States is tried, the Chief Justice shall preside: And no person shall be convicted without the concurrence of two-thirds of the members present.

Judgment in cases of impeachment shall not extend further than to removal from office, and disqualification to hold and enjoy any office of honor, trust or profit under the United States: but the party convicted shall nevertheless be liable and subject to indictment, trial, judgment and punishment, according to law.

Section 4. The times, places and manner of holding elections for Senators and Representatives, shall be prescribed in each state by the legislature thereof; but the Congress may at any time by law make or alter such regulations, except as to the places of choosing Senators.

The Congress shall assemble at least once in every year, and such meeting shall be on the first Monday in December, unless they shall by law appoint a different day.

Section 5. Each House shall be the judge of the elections, returns and qualifications of its own members, and a majority of each shall constitute a quorum to do business; but a smaller number may adjourn from day to day, and may be authorized to compel the attendance of absent members, in such manner, and under such penalties as each House may provide.

Each House may determine the rules of its proceedings, punish its members for disorderly behaviour, and, with the concurrence of two-thirds, expel a member.

Each House shall keep a journal of its proceedings, and from time to time publish the same, excepting such parts as may in their judgment require secrecy; and the yeas and nays of the members of either House on any question shall, at the desire of one-fifth of those present, be entered on the journal.

Neither House, during the session of Congress, shall, without the consent of the other, adjourn for more than three days, nor to any other place than that in which the two Houses shall be sitting.

Section 6. The Senators and Representatives shall receive a compensation for their services, to be ascertained by law, and paid out of the Treasury of the United States. They shall in all cases, except treason, felony and breach of the peace, be privileged from arrest during their attendance at the session of their respective Houses, and in going to and returning from the same; and for any speech or debate in either House, they shall not be questioned in any other place.

No Senator or Representative shall, during the time for which he was elected, be appointed to any civil office under the authority of the United States, which shall have been created, or the emoluments whereof shall have been increased during such time; and no person holding any office under the United States, shall be a member of either House during his continuance in office.

Section 7. All bills for raising revenue shall originate in the House of Representatives; but the Senate may propose or concur with amendments as on other bills.

Every bill which shall have passed the House of Representatives and the Senate, shall, before it becomes a law, be presented to the President of the United States; if he approves he shall sign it, but if not he shall return it, with his objections to that House in which it shall have originated, who shall enter the objections at large on their journal, and proceed to reconsider it. If after such reconsideration two thirds of that House shall agree to pass the bill, it shall be sent, together with the objections, to the other House, by which it shall likewise be reconsidered, and if approved by two thirds of that House, it shall become a law. But in all such cases the votes of both Houses shall be determined by yeas and nays, and the names of the persons voting for and against the bill shall be entered on the journal of each House respectively. If any bill shall not be returned by the President within ten days (Sundays excepted) after it shall have been presented to him, the same shall be a law, in like manner as if he had signed it, unless the Congress by their adjournment prevent its return, in which case it shall not be a law.

Every order, resolution, or vote to which the concurrence of the Senate and House of Representatives may be necessary (except on a question of adjournment) shall be presented to the Presi-

dent of the United States; and before the same shall take effect, shall be approved by him, or being disapproved by him, shall be repassed by two thirds of the Senate and House of Representatives, according to the rules and limitations prescribed in the case of a bill.

Section 8. The Congress shall have power to lay and collect taxes, duties, imposts and excises, to pay the debts and provide for the common defense and general welfare of the United States; but all duties, imposts and excises shall be uniform throughout the United States;

To borrow money on the credit of the United States;

To regulate commerce with foreign nations, and among the several States, and with the Indian tribes;

To establish a uniform rule of naturalization, and uniform laws on the subject of bankruptcies throughout the United States;

To coin money, regulate the value thereof, and of foreign coin, and fix the standard of weights and measures;

To provide for the punishment of counterfeiting the securities and current coin of the United States;

To establish post offices and post roads;

To promote the progress of science and useful arts, by securing for limited times to authors and inventors the exclusive right to their respective writings and discoveries;

To constitute tribunals inferior to the Supreme Court;

To define and punish piracies and felonies committed on the high seas, and offenses against the law of nations;

To declare war, grant letters of marque and reprisal, and make rules concerning captures on land and water;

To raise and support armies, but no appropriation of money to that use shall be for a longer term than two years;

To provide and maintain a Navy;

To make rules for the government and regulation of the land and naval forces;

To provide for calling forth the militia to execute the laws of the Union, suppress insurrections and repel invasions;

To provide for organizing, arming, and disciplining, the militia, and for governing such part of them as may be employed in the service of the United States, reserving to the states respectively, the appointment of the officers, and the authority of training the militia according to the discipline prescribed by Congress;

To exercise exclusive legislation in all cases whatsoever, over such District (not exceeding ten miles square) as may, by cession of particular states, and the acceptance of Congress, become the seat of the government of the United States, and to exercise like authority over all places purchased by the consent of the legislature of the state in which the same shall be, for the erection of forts, magazines, arsenals, dock-yards, and other needful buildings;—and

To make all laws which shall be necessary and proper for carrying into execution the foregoing powers, and all other powers vested by this Constitution in the government of the United States, or in any department or officer thereof.

Section 9. The migration or importation of such persons as any of the states now existing shall think proper to admit, shall not be prohibited by the Congress prior to the year one thousand eight hundred and eight, but a tax or duty may be imposed on such importation, not exceeding ten dollars for each person.

The privilege of the writ of habeas corpus shall not be suspended, unless when in cases of rebellion or invasion the public safety may require it.

No bill of attainder or ex post facto law shall be passed.

No capitation, or other direct, tax shall be laid, unless in proportion to the census or enumeration herein before directed to be taken.

No tax or duty shall be laid on articles exported from any state.

No preference shall be given by any regulation of commerce or revenue to the ports of one state over those of another: nor shall vessels bound to, or from, one state, be obliged to enter, clear, or pay duties in another.

No money shall be drawn from the Treasury, but in consequence of appropriations made by law; and a regular statement and account of the receipts and expenditures of all public money shall be published from time to time.

No title of nobility shall be granted by the United States: And no person holding any office of profit or trust under them, shall, without the

consent of the Congress, accept of any present, emolument, office, or title, of any kind whatever, from any King, Prince, or foreign state.

Section 10. No state shall enter into any treaty, alliance, or confederation; grant letters of marque and reprisal; coin money; emit bills of credit; make any thing but gold and silver coin a tender in payment of debts; pass any bill of attainder, ex post facto law, or law impairing the obligation of contracts, or grant any title of nobility.

No state shall, without the consent of the Congress, lay any imposts or duties on imports or exports, except what may be absolutely necessary for executing its inspection laws: and the net produce of all duties and imposts, laid by any state on imports or exports, shall be for the use of the Treasury of the United States; and all such laws shall be subject to the revision and control of the Congress.

No state shall, without the consent of Congress, lay any duty of tonnage, keep troops, or ships of war in time of peace, enter into any agreement or compact with another state, or with a foreign power, or engage in war, unless actually invaded, or in such imminent danger as will not admit of delay.

Article II

Section 1. The executive power shall be vested in a President of the United States of America. He shall hold his office during the term of four years, and, together with the Vice President, chosen for the same term, be elected, as follows:

Each state, shall appoint, in such manner as the legislature thereof may direct, a number of electors, equal to the whole number of Senators and Representatives to which the state may be entitled in the Congress; but no Senator or Representative, or person holding an office of trust or profit under the United States, shall be appointed an elector.

The electors shall meet in their respective states, and vote by ballot for two persons, of whom one at least shall not be an inhabitant of the same state with themselves. And they shall make a list of all the persons voted for, and of the number of votes for each; which list they shall sign and certify, and transmit sealed to the seat of the government of the United States, directed to the President of the Senate. The President of the Senate

shall, in the presence of the Senate and House of Representatives, open all the certificates, and the votes shall then be counted. The person having the greatest number of votes shall be the President, if such number be a majority of the whole number of electors appointed; and if there be more than one who have such majority, and have an equal number of votes, then the House of Representatives shall immediately choose by ballot one of them for President; and if no person have a majority, then from the five highest on the list the said House shall in like manner choose the President. But in choosing the President, the votes shall be taken by states, the representation from each state having one vote; a quorum for this purpose shall consist of a member or members from two thirds of the states, and a majority of all the states shall be necessary to a choice.

In every case, after the choice of the President, the person having the greatest number of votes of the electors shall be the Vice President. But if there should remain two or more who have equal votes, the Senate shall choose from them by ballot the Vice President.

The Congress may determine the time of choosing the electors, and the day on which they shall give their votes; which day shall be the same throughout the United States.

No person except a natural born citizen, or a citizen of the United States, at the time of the adoption of this Constitution, shall be eligible to the office of President; neither shall any person be eligible to that office who shall not have attained to the age of thirty-five years, and been fourteen years a resident within the United States.

In case of the removal of the President from office, or of his death, resignation, or inability to discharge the powers and duties of the said office, the same shall devolve on the Vice President, and the Congress may by law provide for the case of removal, death, resignation, or inability, both of the President and Vice President, declaring what officer shall then act as President, and such officer shall act accordingly, until the disability be removed, or a President shall be elected.

The President shall, at stated times, receive for his services, a compensation, which shall neither be increased nor diminished during the period for which he shall have been elected, and he shall not

receive within that period any other emolument from the United States, or any of them.

Before he enters on the execution of his office, he shall take the following oath or affirmation:—"I do solemnly swear (or affirm) that I will faithfully execute the office of President of the United States, and will to the best of my ability, preserve, protect and defend the Constitution of the United States."

Section 2. The President shall be commander in chief of the Army and Navy of the United States, and of the militia of the several States, when called into the actual service of the United States; he may require the opinion, in writing, of the principal officer in each of the executive departments, upon any subject relating to the duties of their respective offices, and he shall have power to grant reprieves and pardons for offenses against the United States, except in cases of impeachment.

He shall have power, by and with the advice and consent of the Senate, to make treaties, provided two thirds of the Senators present concur; and he shall nominate, and by and with the advice and consent of the Senate, shall appoint ambassadors, other public ministers and consuls, judges of the Supreme Court, and all other officers of the United States, whose appointments are not herein otherwise provided for, and which shall be established by law: but the Congress may by law vest the appointment of such inferior officers, as they think proper, in the President alone, in the courts of law, or in the heads of departments.

The President shall have power to fill up all vacancies that may happen during the recess of the Senate, by granting commissions which shall expire at the end of their next session.

Section 3. He shall from time to time give to the Congress information of the state of the Union, and recommend to their consideration such measures as he shall judge necessary and expedient; he may, on extraordinary occasions, convene both Houses, or either of them, and in case of disagreement between them, with respect to the time of adjournment, he may adjourn them to such time as he shall think proper; he shall receive ambassadors and other public ministers; he shall take care that the laws be faithfully executed, and shall commission all the officers of the United States.

Section 4. The President, Vice President and all civil officers of the United States, shall be removed from office on impeachment for, and conviction of, treason, bribery, or other high crimes and misdemeanors.

Article III

Section 1. The judicial power of the United States, shall be vested in one Supreme Court, and in such inferior courts as the Congress may from time to time ordain and establish. The judges, both of the supreme and inferior courts, shall hold their offices during good behaviour, and shall, at stated times, receive for their services, a compensation, which shall not be diminished during their continuance in office.

Section 2. The judicial power shall extend to all cases, in law and equity, arising under this Constitution, the laws of the United States, and treaties made, or which shall be made, under their authority;—to all cases affecting ambassadors, other public ministers and consuls;—to all cases of admiralty and maritime jurisdiction;—to controversies to which the United States shall be a party;—to controversies between two or more states;—between a state and citizens of another state;—between citizens of different states,—between citizens of the same state claiming lands under grants of different states, and between a state, or the citizens thereof, and foreign states, citizens or subjects.

In all cases affecting ambassadors, other public ministers and consuls, and those in which a state shall be a party, the Supreme Court shall have original jurisdiction. In all the other cases before mentioned, the Supreme Court shall have appellate jurisdiction, both as to law and fact, with such exceptions, and under such regulations as the Congress shall make.

The trial of all crimes, except in cases of impeachment, shall be by jury; and such trial shall be held in the state where the said crimes shall have been committed; but when not committed within any state, the trial shall be at such place or places as the Congress may by law have directed.

Section 3. Treason against the United States, shall consist only in levying war against them, or in adhering to their enemies, giving them aid and comfort. No person shall be convicted of treason unless on the testimony of two witnesses to the same overt act, or on confession in open court.

The Congress shall have power to declare the punishment of treason, but no attainder of treason shall work corruption of blood, or forfeiture except during the life of the person attained.

Article IV

Section 1. Full faith and credit shall be given in each state to the public acts, records, and judicial proceedings of every other state. And the Congress may by general laws prescribe the manner in which such acts, records and proceedings shall be proved, and the effect thereof.

Section 2. The citizens of each state shall be entitled to all privileges and immunities of citizens in the several states.

A person charged in any state with treason, felony, or other crime, who shall flee from justice, and be found in another state, shall on demand of the executive authority of the state from which he fled, be delivered up, to be removed to the state having jurisdiction of the crime.

No person held to service or labour in one state, under the laws thereof, escaping into another, shall, in consequence of any law or regulation therein, be discharged from such service or labour, but shall be delivered up on claim of the party to whom such service or labour may be due.

Section 3. New states may be admitted by the Congress into this Union; but no new state shall be formed or erected within the jurisdiction of any other state; nor any state be formed by the junction of two or more states, or parts of states, without the consent of the legislature of the states concerned as well as of the Congress.

The Congress shall have power to dispose of and make all needful rules and regulations respecting the territory or other property belonging to the United States; and nothing in this Constitution shall be so construed as to prejudice any claims of the United States, or of any particular state.

Section 4. The United States shall guarantee to every state in this Union a republican form of government, and shall protect each of them against invasion; and on application of the legislature, or of the executive (when the legislature cannot be convened) against domestic violence.

Article V

The Congress, whenever two thirds of both Houses shall deem it necessary, shall propose amendments to this Constitution, or on the application of the legislatures of two thirds of the several states, shall call a convention for proposing amendments, which, in either case, shall be valid to all intents and purposes, as part of this Constitution, when ratified by the legislatures of three fourths of the several States, or by conventions in three fourths thereof, as the one or the other mode of ratification may be proposed by the Congress; provided that no amendment which may be made prior to the year one thousand eight hundred and eight shall in any manner affect the first and fourth clauses in the Ninth Section of the First Article; and that no state, without its consent, shall be deprived of its equal suffrage in the Senate.

Article VI

All debts contracted and engagements entered into, before the adoption of this Constitution, shall be as valid against the United States under this Constitution, as under the Confederation.

This Constitution, and the laws of the United States which shall be made in pursuance thereof; and all treaties made, or which shall be made, under the authority of the United States, shall be the supreme law of the land; and the judges in every state shall be bound thereby, any thing in the Constitution or laws of any State to the contrary notwithstanding.

The Senators and Representatives before mentioned, and the members of the several state legislatures, and all executive and judicial officers, both of the United States and of the several states, shall be bound by oath or affirmation, to support this Constitution; but no religious test shall ever be required as a qualification to any office or public trust under the United States.

Article VII

The ratification of the conventions of nine states shall be sufficient for the establishment of this Constitution between the states so ratifying the same.

Done in convention by the unanimous consent of the states present the seventeenth day of September in the year of our Lord one thousand seven

hundred and eighty seven and of the independence of the United States of America the twelfth. In witness whereof we have hereunto subscribed our names,

Go. WASHINGTON—*Presid't,*
and deputy from Virginia
Attest WILLIAM JACKSON *Secretary*

New Hampshire
JOHN LANGDON   NICHOLAS GILMAN

Massachusetts
NATHANIEL GORHAM   RUFUS KING

Connecticut
WM. SAML. JOHNSON   ROGER SHERMAN

New York
ALEXANDER HAMILTON

New Jersey
WIL: LIVINGSTON   WM. PATERSON
DAVID BREARLEY   JONA: DAYTON

Pennsylvania
B FRANKLIN   THOS. FITZSIMONS
THOMAS MIFFLIN   JARED INGERSOLL
ROBT MORRIS   JAMES WILSON
GEO. CLYMER   GOUV MORRIS

Delaware
GEO: READ   RICHARD BASSETT
GUNNING BEDFORD JUN   JACO: BROOM
JOHN DICKINSON

Maryland
JAMES MCHENRY   DANL CARROLL
DAN OF ST THOS.
  JENIFER

Virginia
JOHN BLAIR—   JAMES MADISON JR.

North Carolina
WM. BLOUNT   HU WILLIAMSON
RICHD. DOBBS SPAIGHT

South Carolina
J. RUTLEDGE   CHARLES PINCKNEY
CHARLES COTESWORTH   PIERCE BUTLER
  PINCKNEY

Georgia
WILLIAM FEW   ABR BALDWIN

Amendments

Article I (1791)

Congress shall make no law respecting an establishment of religion, or prohibiting the free exercise thereof; or abridging the freedom of speech, or of the press; or the right of the people peaceably to assemble, and to petition the government for a redress of grievances.

Article II (1791)

A well-regulated militia, being necessary to the security of a free state, the right of the people to keep and bear arms, shall not be infringed.

Article III (1791)

No soldier shall, in time of peace be quartered in any house, without the consent of the owner, nor in time of war, but in a manner to be prescribed by law.

Article IV (1791)

Tht right of the people to be secure in their persons, houses, papers, and effects, against unreasonable searches and seizures, shall not be violated, and no warrants shall issue, but upon probable cause, supported by oath or affirmation, and particularly describing the place to be searched, and the persons or things to be seized.

Article V (1791)

No person shall be held to answer for a capital, or otherwise infamous crime, unless on a presentment or indictment of a Grand Jury, except in cases arising in the land or naval forces, or in the militia, when in actual service in time of war or public danger; nor shall any person be subject for the same offense to be twice put in jeopardy of life or limb; nor shall be compelled in any criminal case to be a witness against himself, nor be deprived of life, liberty, or property, without due process of law; nor shall private property be taken for public use, without just compensation.

Article VI (1791)

In all criminal prosecutions, the accused shall enjoy the right to a speedy and public trial, by an impartial jury of the state and district wherein the crime shall have been committed, which district shall have been previously ascertained by law, and to be informed of the nature and cause of the accusation; to be confronted with the witnesses against him; to have compulsory process for obtaining witnesses in his favor, and to have the assistance of counsel for his defense.

Article VII (1791)

In suits at common law, where the value in controversy shall exceed twenty dollars, the right of trial by jury shall be preserved, and no fact tried by a jury, shall be otherwise reexamined in any court of the United States, than according to the rules of the common law.

Article VIII (1791)

Excessive bail shall not be required, nor excessive fines imposed, nor cruel and unusual punishments inflicted.

Article IX (1791)

The enumeration in the Constitution, of certain rights, shall not be construed to deny or disparage others retained by the people.

Article X (1791)

The powers not delegated to the United States by the Constitution, nor prohibited by it to the states, are reserved to the states respectively, or to the people.

Article XI (1795)

The judicial power of the United States shall not be construed to extend to any suit in law or equity, commenced or prosecuted against one of the United States by citizens of another state, or by citizens or subjects of any foreign state.

Article XII (1804)

The electors shall meet in their respective states, and vote by ballot for President and Vice President, one of whom, at least, shall not be an inhabitant of the same state with themselves; they shall name in their ballots the person voted for as President, and in distinct ballots the person voted for as Vice President, and they shall make distinct lists of all persons voted for as President, and of all persons voted for as Vice President, and of the number of votes for each, which lists they shall sign and certify, and transmit sealed to the seat of the government of the United States, directed to the President of the Senate;—The President of the Senate shall, in the presence of the Senate and House of Representatives, open all the certificates and the votes shall then be counted;—The person having the greatest number of votes for President, shall be the President, if such number be a majority of the whole number of electors appointed; and if no person have such majority, then from the persons having the highest numbers not exceeding three on the list of those voted for as President, the House of Representatives shall choose immediately, by ballot, the President. But in choosing the President, the votes shall be taken by states, the representation from each state having one vote; a quorum for this purpose shall consist of a member or members from two-thirds of the states, and a majority of all the states shall be necessary to a choice. And if the House of Representatives shall not choose a President whenever the right of choice shall devolve upon them, before the fourth day of March next following, then the Vice President shall act as President, as in the case of the death or other constitutional disability of the President.—The person having the greatest number of votes as Vice President, shall be the Vice President, if such number be a majority of the whole number of electors appointed, and if no person have a majority, then from the two highest numbers on the list, the Senate shall choose the Vice President; a quorum for the purpose shall consist of two-thirds of the whole number of Senators, and a majority of the whole number shall be necessary to a choice. But no person constitutionally ineligible to the office of President shall be eligible to that of Vice President of the United States.

Article XIII (1865)

Section 1. Neither slavery nor involuntary servitude, except as a punishment for crime whereof the party shall have been duly convicted, shall exist within the United States, or any place subject to their jurisdiction.

Section 2. Congress shall have power to enforce this article by appropriate legislation.

Article XIV (1868)

Section 1. All persons born or naturalized in the United States, and subject to the jurisdiction thereof, are citizens of the United States and of the state wherein they reside. No state shall make or enforce any law which shall abridge the privileges or immunities of citizens of the United States; nor shall any state deprive any person of life, liberty, or property, without due process of law; nor deny to any person within its jurisdiction the equal protection of the laws.

Section 2. Representatives shall be apportioned among the several states according to their respective numbers, counting the whole number of persons in each state, excluding Indians not taxed. But when the right to vote at any election for the choice of electors for President and Vice President of the United States, Representatives in Congress, the executive and judicial officers of a state, or the members of the legislature thereof, is denied to any of the male inhabitants of such state, being twenty-one years of age, and citizens of the United States, or in any way abridged, except for participation in rebellion, or other crime, the basis of representation therein shall be reduced in the proportion which the number of such male citizens shall bear to the whole number of male citizens twenty-one years of age in such state.

Section 3. No person shall be a Senator or Representative in Congress, or elector of President and Vice President, or hold any office, civil or military, under the United States, or under any state, who, having previously taken an oath, as a member of Congress, or as an officer of the United States, or as a member of any state legislature, or as an executive or judicial officer of any state, to support the Constitution of the United States, shall have engaged in insurrection or rebellion against the same, or given aid or comfort to the

enemies thereof. But Congress may by a vote of two-thirds of each house, remove such disability.

Section 4. The validity of the public debt of the United States, authorized by law, including debts incurred for payment of pensions and bounties for services in suppressing insurrection or rebellion, shall not be questioned. But neither the United States nor any state shall assume or pay any debt or obligation incurred in aid of insurrection or rebellion against the United States, or any claim for the loss or emancipation of any slave; but all such debts, obligations and claims shall be held illegal and void.

Section 5. The Congress shall have power to enforce, by appropriate legislation, the provisions of this article.

Article XV (1870)

Section 1. The right of citizens of the United States to vote shall not be denied or abridged by the United States or by any state on account of race, color, or previous condition of servitude.

Section 2. The Congress shall have power to enforce this article by appropriate legislation.

Article XVI (1913)

The Congress shall have power to lay and collect taxes on incomes, from whatever source derived, without apportionment among the several states, and without regard to any census or enumeration.

Article XVII (1913)

Section 1. The Senate of the United States shall be composed of two Senators from each state, elected by the people thereof, for six years; and each Senator shall have one vote. The electors in each state shall have the qualifications requisite for electors of the most numerous branch of the state legislature.

Section 2. When vacancies happen in the representation of any state in the Senate, the executive authority of such state shall issue writs of election to fill such vacancies: *Provided*, That the legislature of any state may empower the executive thereof to make temporary appointments until the people fill the vacancies by election as the legislature may direct.

Section 3. This amendment shall not be so construed as to affect the election or term of any Senator chosen before it becomes valid as part of the Constitution.

Article XVIII (1919)

Section 1. After one year from the ratification of this article the manufacture, sale, or transportation of intoxicating liquors within, the importation thereof into, or the exportation thereof from the United States and all territory subject to the jurisdiction thereof for beverage purposes is hereby prohibited.

Section 2. The Congress and the several states shall have concurrent power to enforce this article by appropriate legislation.

Section 3. This article shall be inoperative unless it shall have been ratified as an amendment to the Constitution by the legislatures of the several states, as provided in the Constitution, within seven years from the date of the submission hereof to the states by the Congress.

Article XIX (1920)

Section 1. The right of citizens of the United States to vote shall not be denied or abridged by the United States or by any state on account of sex.

Section 2. Congress shall have power to enforce this article by appropriate legislation.

Article XX (1933)

Section 1. The terms of the President and Vice President shall end at noon on the 20th day of January, and the terms of Senators and Representatives at noon on the 3d day of January, of the years in which such terms would have ended if this article had not been ratified; and the terms of their successors shall then begin.

Section 2. The Congress shall assemble at least once in every year, and such meeting shall begin at noon on the 3d day of January, unless they shall by law appoint a different day.

Section 3. If, at the time fixed for the beginning of the term of the President, the President elect shall have died, the Vice President elect shall become President. If a President shall not have

been chosen before the time fixed for the beginning of his term, or if the President elect shall have failed to qualify, then the Vice President elect shall act as President until a President shall have qualified; and the Congress may by law provide for the case wherein neither a President elect nor a Vice President elect shall have qualified, declaring who shall then act as President, or the manner in which one who is to act shall be selected, and such person shall act accordingly until a President or Vice President shall have qualified.

Section 4. The Congress may by law provide for the case of the death of any of the persons from whom the House of Representatives may choose a President whenever the right of choice shall have devolved upon them, and for the case of the death of any of the persons from whom the Senate may choose a Vice President whenever the right of choice shall have devolved upon them.

Section 5. Sections 1 and 2 shall take effect on the 15th day of October following the ratification of this article.

Section 6. This article shall be inoperative unless it shall have been ratified as an amendment to the Constitution by the legislatures of three-fourths of the several states within seven years from the date of its submission.

Article XXI (1933)

Section 1. The eighteenth article of amendment to the Constitution of the United States is hereby repealed.

Section 2. The transportation or importation into any state, territory, or possession of the United States for delivery or use therein of intoxicating liquors, in violation of the laws thereof, is hereby prohibited.

Section 3. This article shall be inoperative unless it shall have been ratified as an amendment to the Constitution by conventions in the several states, as provided in the Constitution, within seven years from the date of the submission hereof to the states by the Congress.

Article XXII (1951)

Section 1. No person shall be elected to the office of the President more than twice, and no person who has held the office of President, or acted as President, for more than two years of a term

to which some other person was elected President shall be elected to the office of the President more than once. But this Article shall not apply to any person holding the office of President when this Article was proposed by the Congress, and shall not prevent any person who may be holding the office of President, or acting as President, during the term within which this Article becomes operative from holding the office of President or acting as President during the remainder of such term.

Section 2. This Article shall be inoperative unless it shall have been ratified as an amendment to the Constitution by the legislatures of three-fourths of the several states within seven years from the date of its submission to the states by the Congress.

Article XXIII (1961)

Section 1. The District constituting the seat of government of the United States shall appoint in such manner as the Congress may direct:

A number of electors of President and Vice President equal to the whole number of Senators and Representatives in Congress to which the District would be entitled if it were a state, but in no event more than the least populous state; they shall be in addition to those appointed by the states, but they shall be considered, for the purposes of the election of President and Vice President, to be electors appointed by a state; and they shall meet in the District and perform such duties as provided by the twelfth article of amendment.

Section 2. The Congress shall have power to enforce this article by appropriate legislation.

Article XXIV (1964)

Section 1. The right of citizens of the United States to vote in any primary or other election for President or Vice President, for electors for President or Vice President, or for Senator or Representative in Congress, shall not be denied or abridged by the United States or any State by reason of failure to pay any poll tax or other tax.

Section 2. The Congress shall have power to enforce this article by appropriate legislation.

Article XXV (1967)

Section 1. In case of the removal of the President from office or of his death or resignation, the Vice President shall become President.

Section 2. Whenever there is a vacancy in the office of the Vice President, the President shall nominate a Vice President who shall take office upon confirmation by a majority vote of both Houses of Congress.

Section 3. Whenever the President transmits to the President pro tempore of the Senate and the Speaker of the House of Representatives his written declaration that he is unable to discharge the powers and duties of his office, and until he transmits to them a written declaration to the contrary, such powers and duties shall be discharged by the Vice President as Acting President.

Section 4. Whenever the Vice President and a majority of either the principal officers of the executive departments or of such other body as Congress may by law provide, transmit to the President pro tempore of the Senate and the Speaker of the House of Representatives their written declaration that the President is unable to discharge the powers and duties of his office, the Vice President shall immediately assume the powers and duties of the office as Acting President.

Thereafter, when the President transmits to the President pro tempore of the Senate and the Speaker of the House of Representatives his written declaration that no inability exists, he shall resume the powers and duties of his office unless the Vice President and a majority of either the principal officers of the executive department or of such other body as Congress may by law provide, transmit within four days to the President pro tempore of the Senate and the Speaker of the House of Representatives their written declaration that the President is unable to discharge the powers and duties of his office. Thereupon Congress shall decide the issue, assemblying within forty-eight hours for that purpose if not in session. If the Congress, within twenty-one days after receipt of the latter written declaration, or, if Congress is not in session, within twenty-one days after Congress is required to assemble, determines by two-thirds vote of both Houses that the President is unable to discharge the powers and duties of his office, the Vice President shall continue to discharge the same as Acting President; otherwise, the President shall resume the powers and duties of his office.

Article XXVI (1971)

Section 1. The right of citizens of the United States, who are eighteen years of age or older, to vote shall not be denied or abridged by the United States or by any State on account of age.

Section 2. The Congress shall have power to enforce this article by appropriate legislation.